Cashflow
Cookbook

Canadian Edition

Cashflow Cookbook

Canadian Edition

$2 Million of Financial Freedom
in 60 Easy Recipes

Gordon Stein

CFCB Press

Published by CFCB Inc.
Toronto
CashflowCookbook.com

ISBN: 978-1-77519-540-5

Fifth printing

Developmental editing by Elizabeth Williams
Copy edited by Donna Dawson, CPE
Cover designed by Angie at pro_ebookcovers and Scott Kish
Page layout by Sheila Mahoney

Important Note to Readers
The contents of this book are for general information only. This book presents ideas for handling many situations that may require a professional advisor, counsellor, technician or tradesperson (an "expert"). This book is not a substitute for the involvement of an expert in your specific situation. Before applying general information to your own situation, always consult an expert with the qualifications needed in your circumstances. Failure to do so may result in harm. The author is writing based on his own experience. Applying the author's ideas and experience to your specific situation may produce results that differ from the author's results. Results may vary from person to person. This book is not intended to solicit the sale of any investment or financial or insurance product. Any similarity or resemblance of characters to persons living or deceased in any of the anecdotes or scenarios presented is purely coincidental.

Dedicated to the memory of my mother, Thelma Barer-Stein, who gave me a lifelong love of learning, reading and writing.

Contents

Introduction 1

Housing 20

    Shish Kebabed Home Insurance 21

    Home Alarm Hash 24

    Glazed Snow Removal with a Side of Frozen Fingerlings 27

    Gas Bill Gumbo 30

    Electric Bill Braised in a Juice Reduction 34

    Home Furnishing Fricassee 38

    Marinated Mortgage Rate on Rye 41

    Mortgage Life Insurance Mousse 45

    Home Repair Ratatouille 48

    Self-Storage Sashimi 51

    The Take-Away Container 54

Cars & Transportation 55

    Traffic-Beating Beets 56

    Car Wash Clafouti 59

    Traffic Ticket Tikka Masala 62

    Car Insurance Clam Bake with Steamed Radiator 65

    Devilled Driving Habits 68

    Mall Trip Meringue 71

    Car Repair Ragout 74

    Layered Commute Parfait 77

    SUV Succotash 80

    Parking Lot Perogies 83

    The Take-Away Container 86

Food & Drink 87

    Battered Bottled Water 88

    Big-Brand Bourguignon on a Bed of Je Ne Sais Quoi 91

    Frozen Food Frittata 94

    Prepared Food Purée 97

    Meat Reduction Marinara 100

    Sale Bin Salsa 103

    Grocery List Ganache 106

    Sweet & Sour Snacks in a Belly Fat Confit 109

    Packed Lunch Lyonnaise 112

    Detox Drinks du Jour 115

    The Take-Away Container 118

Household 119

Dry Cleaning Demi-Glace 120
Shaved Blade Roast 123
Stewed Sports Spending 126
Haircut Mousse with all the Trimmings 129
Par-Boiled Prescriptions 132
Trussed and Roasted Clothing Costs 135
Seared Cell Service 138
Lean Ground Learning 141
Post-Secondary Pot Roast 144
Deep-Fried Day Care with Blanched Budget 147
The Take-Away Container 150
Lifestyle 152
Music Mincemeat 153
Reading Ravioli 156
Diced Salsa with Chips 159
Night Out à la Mode 162
Julienne of Gym Costs in a Light Sweat Sauce 165
Video Vichyssoise 168
Travel Bill Tostada 171
Time-Off Trappings Tofu 174
Char-Broiled Restaurant Cheques 177
Smoked Cigarettes in a Blackened Lung Sauce 180
The Take-Away Container 183
Financial 185
Cashflow Leeks with Fresh-Squeezed Bank Fees 186
Fine-Print Filet with a Credit Card Chiffonade 189
Lightly Poached Life Insurance 193
Tax Refund Tartar with Deduction Extract 196
Refried RESP 199
Diced Debt in an Interest Rate Infusion 202
Chicken-Fried Foreign Exchange with Nest Egg Gravy 206
Benefits Bourguignon Simmered in Stock 210
Sparkling Investment Returns in a Low-Cost Sauce 213
Second Income Sabayon 222
The Take-Away Container 225
Overall Summary: The Stock Pot 226
Epilogue 227
Cashflow Cookbook: The Website 229
Acknowledgements 231
Public Speaking 232

Introduction

PERSONAL FINANCE. BUDGETING. Saving. Ugh.

Hands up if you think you have this all locked down. Raise your other hand if you find this stuff fun at all. That's what I thought.

If you struggle with money, are trying to save for retirement or have dreams of financial independence, this book is for you.

Cashflow Cookbook offers a new approach to financial freedom: 60 easy recipes that anyone can use to reduce their spending with minimal sacrifice of time and lifestyle, all as easy as, well, following a recipe.

The recipes each take between 10 minutes and a couple of hours to implement and can save between $25 and $900 *each month*. Investing those savings can provide more than **$700,000** over 10 years for a single person and over **$2 million** for a family.

Yes, really.

Is This Book for You?

Cashflow Cookbook is an ideal resource for

- **Job hunters** who need to stretch out a severance package
- **Teachers** who help students learn about finances
- **Couples** who spend too much time fighting about money

- **Retirees** trying to maximize their spending power
- **The newly divorced**, coping with starting over
- **Families** trying to reduce money worries
- **Entrepreneurs** who need to keep expenses lean
- **Graduates** paying loans as they enter the workforce
- **Anyone** who is tired of trying to keep a budget and wants an easier way to financial independence

As fun and useful as this book may be for many people, I'd like to be clear that it's not for everyone.

If you bought a copy for some light reading in your private jet en route to a polo match in Dubai, you may have squandered the purchase price. Leave the book in the airport for someone else to enjoy.

If your income is under about $40,000, you may find that some of the material doesn't apply. Don't be put off. Sample the rest of the buffet. You will still find some dishes to your taste.

Some people need more financial help than this book can offer. *Seek professional help if you*

- Are addicted to shopping and literally cannot hold onto your credit cards as you pass a store
- Have amassed a large amount of credit card debt and the balance is out of control
- Are dealing with significant emotional stress due to your spending and it is affecting your sleep or relationships
- Are dealing with creditors calling every day and don't know how to make them stop
- Have amassed gambling debts or there are people seeking to do you grievous harm

It Began with a Car Wash

Many years back, I was driving to a party with a friend, Peter. He spotted a car wash receipt on the floor mat and asked why I would spend money on car washes. I think I explained that I didn't want to spend my weekends washing my car by hand. Whatever I said, the real reason was that I couldn't be bothered to worry about the cost of car washes.

That would change.

Peter went on to explain how the points he earned through a gas retailer loyalty program got him free car washes. I nodded, but seriously, was I really going to sign up for the program, remember to swipe my loyalty card, go online somewhere to track points and then fill in some form, all to collect a free wash? Then there was the issue of carrying one of those monster wallets stuffed with loyalty cards for every fish market, haircutting place and oil change shop. Who needs it?

Fast forward a few years. I'm sitting in the sombre confines of an outplacement firm. Things came into sharp focus as bills arrived but a finite number of months remained on my severance package. Stretching X months of money into Y months of living became a bit of a mission.

As I got to know my fellow outplacement inmates it was clear that financials were suddenly a big deal for us. People were pondering selling their cottages, cancelling their kids' programs and looking for ways to stretch their grocery budget.

Driving to the outplacement office one day, I heard an ad for a discount home alarm company. The catchy jingle caught my attention—their price was about $25 cheaper each month than what I was paying. Hmm.

I remembered Peter's car wash idea, worth about the same $25 per month. I signed up for the gas loyalty program that day, and then called the alarm company. Between the two, my chequing account was fatter by $50 a month.

OK, sure, it was only 50 bucks. And I would still need to find a job. But it was also incredibly easy. I got a gas card for my wife and we saved another $25 a month. With minimal effort, we now had $75 each month of real savings.

I then did a bit of math to see how $75 a month might grow if I invested it at, say, 7%, for 10 years. Incredibly, the answer was $12,975. I began to wonder what else could drive easy savings. If there were enough of them, could they amount to real money? Could these simple ideas be the ticket to financial freedom?

Help Is at Hand

Over the next few years, I gathered the best of these ideas into a spreadsheet and did the math to figure out what the savings would amount to over the years. Some saved as much as $900 per month. I realized these ideas could help a lot of people.

And help seems to be needed: we Canadians are not in great financial shape:

- 68% of Canadian divorces are caused by money issues.[1]
- Canadian debt is now 165% of income.[2]
- Among those aged 55–64 with no employer pension, roughly half have savings that represent less than one year's worth of what they need to supplement government retirement income programs.[3]

---

[1] BMO poll, executed by Pollara, online sample of 1,001 Canadians aged 18 and older, Jan 24–28, 2014.
[2] Statistics Canada, June 14, 2016.
[3] Broadbent Institute, Feb 16, 2016.

- 31% of Canadians don't make enough money to cover their bills.[4]
- Only 32% of Canadians with household incomes between $150,000 and $249,000 have maxed out their Tax Free Savings Accounts.[5]
- Only half of Canadian parents are using an RESP to save for their children's education, and only 34% are taking full advantage of the available government grant.[6]
- The average car loan is now 69 months; 96-month loans are increasingly popular.[7]

I read newspaper stories about people choked by debt. I saw payday loan locations popping up everywhere. I even spoke with high-end investment advisors who gave me the clear picture that most of their clients have little actual wealth, even though they drive BMWs, enjoy high-end club memberships and know a good Pinot from one from an "off" year.

I read about the crisis in financial literacy. We have kids graduating from university who can dissect a pig, calculate the strength of covalent bonds, name all the parts of a cell—right down to the endoplasmic reticulum (still my favourite cell part after all these years) and play a mean game of beer pong. But do they know how to manage their finances? Or are they likely to follow in their parents' path of impulse buying, growing debt and the paycheque treadmill?

I spent some time in bookstores and online looking at the financial texts. I saw lots of repackaging of the basic idea of spending less

4 MNP Debt Survey, May 8, 2017.
5 Canada Revenue Agency data as reported in the *National Post* by Garry Marr, May 9, 2013.
6 *BMO Wealth Institute Report*, Canadian Edition, Mar 2013.
7 "Eight-year car loans drive sales and deepen Canadians' debt problems," *Financial Post*, Aug 20, 2017.

than you earn: save 10% of what you make and squirrel that away in savings. Invest in mutual funds—wait, scratch that; go for exchange-traded funds.

But where is that 10% supposed to come from? What if I can't make ends meet as it is? Just when you think you have 10% set aside and that next paycheque is only a couple of days away, it's time to pay for the kids' hockey program. Dang!

My time with the outplacement company convinced me that there are many, many people who live from paycheque to paycheque—one leaky roof or dog surgery away from a financial crisis.

I looked at frugality blogs and read a lot of ideas about how to reduce your cat food expenditures and reuse your J Cloths. One talked about taping tinfoil to your windows to save on air conditioning. Another suggested growing a herb garden. OK, they are ideas, but what kind of savings are they going to amount to? What if I don't want tinfoil on my windows? And how much parsley can I eat in a year? There has to be a better way.

Meanwhile, I had gathered 120 ideas on my spreadsheet. I grouped them into categories and completed the math on what the savings would be worth for a single person or a family invested at 7% over 10 and 20 years.

The total was more than $700,000 for singles and an incredible $2.4 million for a family.

No, the calculations don't consider inflation, but these are still massive numbers. And these are ideas that pretty much everyone can use. They're easy to implement and will return many times what you have spent on this book—all with minimal effort and sacrifice and without onerous budgeting. Tasty indeed.

First, A Few Fundamentals

Before we get cooking, we need to start with some fundamentals. And that includes fixing some bad habits and starting some great new ones—cleaning out your financial fridge, if you will—before attempting new techniques.

Let's look at how to

- Simmer your spending
- Deglaze your debt
- Toss the toxic ingredients
- Noodle your net worth

The Spending Simmer

Retail therapy. Heading to the mall. Clicking that sponsored link in Facebook.

Pull out your last few bank and credit card statements. Is there a pattern? Does the pain of the bills wipe out the fun of the spending? Are you carrying a balance on one or more credit cards? When you think of your personal finances and look at your statements do you feel relaxed or anxious?

If you feel anxious, you are in good company. A multi-billion-dollar consumer machine, run by some very clever people, is constantly trying to convince you to spend what you have.

And then spend what you don't have.

It's a system where everyone wins. Stores sell more products so shareholders make money. Landlords lease more shopping centres. Food courts sell more addictive salt, sugar and fat. The banks feast on the credit card interest. The economy booms. Everyone wins.

Except you.

Let's take one more trip to the mall, but this time leave your cash and cards at home. Really look at the stores and the merchandizing:

the limited time sales, the beautiful lighting, the dizzying array of products. How much of it do we really need? How much of it is there to create a need where none exists? And of course, all of this also applies to the slick online ads, last-minute e-commerce promotions and don't-leave-our-website pop-ups.

Have you ever felt that you are a slave to your things? Moving them out of the way to get to your other things. Storing them. Maintaining them. Buying them thing-accessories. Then sorting and separating the things you need from those you hope to unload at next year's yard sale at five cents on the dollar. And that's before the hagglers arrive.

If you're one of the millions of victims of this insane retail circus, fear not! It's a simple habit to kick. Stay away from the mall unless you actually need something. When you do go, make a list of what you actually need, and buy just those things. It might help to spend a few minutes reading your bank and credit card statements before you go.

Deglazing Debt

Imagine you're making dinner. You measure 300 ml of chicken stock and return the container to the fridge. But then a glance at the measuring cup gives you pause. There are only 100 ml in the cup. How fast can chicken stock evaporate? Weird. You fill the cup back up to 300 ml and move on to chopping 250 ml of onions. As you fill the bowl, a glance at the chicken stock shows it's back down to 100 ml. What the…? And now the bowl of onions is only half full! At this rate, you will never get dinner made. And it will take twice the ingredients. At a minimum.

Carrying debt is like having someone stealing your ingredients as you try to cook. The interest on debt means you're going backward when you're trying to move forward. It causes lost sleep. It limits possibilities. And if anything changes in the household, like an unanticipated expense or a job loss, it can be devastating.

Let's look at an example.

Bruno was living the dream: A great marriage, two fantastic children and a lovely home. They enjoyed summers biking and winters skiing. His wife, Jodi, was busy raising the kids, attending parent-teacher meetings and shuttling the kids to their activities. Bruno had been moving up at the bank where he had worked for more than 25 years. Following his last promotion, he had splurged on leasing a new SUV, the $800 payments well within his earning power.

When Bruno arrived for his regular weekly meeting with his manager one day, he was surprised to see the head of HR there. You can guess what happened next: The large white envelope held the severance package and the conversation was a blur about restructuring, bank profitability, changing trends and new options ahead. He caught an Uber home, his mind a dizzying stream of thoughts, dread and worry.

Over the coming weeks, Bruno worked with his accountant to build a plan. It became apparent that there had been a lot of income—and no shortage of expenditure—but he had very little **net worth**. Although he had built a great career over 25 years, he was hardly more financially secure than he had been a decade earlier. In fact, with the heavy financial drain of car payments, mortgage and club fees, he could quickly move to a point of financial desperation just months after losing his job.

Bruno was able to find a new role at a credit union at a lower salary. Right away, he ditched the SUV for a more modest ride and reduced his other expenses to build net worth and help guard against future financial calamities.

If you wince when the credit card bill arrives, or if you carry a balance, it is time to take a real look at your debt and build a plan to eliminate it forever.

Start by getting all your debts out on the countertop where you can see them. Ouch. It's a bit painful, but it's better than hiding them. Extra honesty points for including that second secret credit card. Have a peek at the tiny print on the statement that covers the interest you pay. Keep looking; it's there somewhere. It's probably something shocking like 21%.

Now build a simple debt sheet like the one below, sorted by interest rate. You can download a debt sheet template from the Utensils section at CashflowCookbook.com.

How Bruno Got His Groove Back

As he started to rebuild his life, Bruno realized he had a shopping cart load of debts pulling his finances backward. While he was working, he didn't worry too much about the interest charges. But with no income, he realized how these debts would keep him working forever and hijack the financial dreams he held for his family.

The plan was to trim the fat from his debts, starting with the highest-interest debt and working his way down the list. Credit card interest at 21% is punishing. Carrying a balance of $3,600 at 21% adds up to $756 a year just in interest (actually more than that due to compounding, but let's keep it simple)—for stuff Bruno likely bought and rarely used. And that is just on one of his debts, as shown below (amounts are rounded for simplicity).

Debt Type	Interest Rate	Balance Owing	Monthly Payment	Annual Interest
Credit card 1	21%	$3,600	$220	$756
Credit card 2	19%	$2,100	$186	$399
Car loan	6%	$6,300	$538	$208
Line of credit	5%	$12,500	$201	$583
Mortgage	4.64%	$327,000	$2,153	$14,793

If we could find Bruno $3,600 we could pay off that first card. That would free up $220 each month, which he could then use to increase the $186 monthly payment on the second card and get rid of that balance too, saving more than $1,000 each year in interest once both are paid off.

If you're carrying credit card debt, declare a full emergency and get it paid off. When you free up some cash with the recipes that follow, start attacking the highest-interest debt; raise the payments to get rid of it sooner. Then go after the next debt, and so on, until they are all gone. Now instead of your debt dragging you backward, you're cooking up savings to pull yourself forward. Imagine your money growing money of its own. Imagine a herb garden where no matter how much you cut, there's always more. How cool is that?

> If you have two credit cards charging about the same interest, start by frying the one with the smaller balance, letting you clear it sooner, and then move on to the bigger one.

Now here's where Bruno turns the corner: By turning down the heat on his spending and reinvesting the savings from paying down one debt into paying down other debts, he is now $1,946 a month richer. If he uses that money to nearly double his mortgage payments he'll eliminate that debt *11 years* earlier than planned. With all the debts gone, he could free up almost $3,100 each month, save a pile of interest and protect his family from future financial kitchen fires.

I know, I know: all of this is great, but where does the money actually come from to do it? Patience, Grasshopper! That's what the recipes are for.

Toss the Toxins

Just as toxins have no place in your food, there are certain things that are just not good to have in your financial pantry. We've already discussed the dangers of carrying credit card debt. Here are a few other poisons to avoid:

- **Using Payday Loans:** Ouch. Payday loans are the junk food of money. You are paying incredible interest rates for the convenience of having money to make it to the next paycheque while chaining yourself to a painful debt cycle. Use the recipes in this book to drive enough savings to break the habit. Start a positive cycle by eliminating this searing interest cost and use that freed-up cash to start getting out of debt.

- **Renting Furniture:** Stop. Do the math. Some furniture rental places charge three times the value of the furniture over a 36- or 48-month period, plus a buyout at the end. Just do without the furniture while saving for a nice used piece from Kijiji or Craigslist. Or check out places offering gently used furniture.

- **Buying Too Much House or Car:** Buy cars gently used to save on depreciation and buy a car that can handle 95% of what you need it for. If you need two cars, consider a small one for commuting if you must and a larger one for family outings. Cars are well built these days and can last 250,000 km or more. The same principle applies with houses. Buy in a good location but not more house than you need.

Net Worth Noodling

David looked down to admire his new belt. But he couldn't see it! Strangely, a gut was covering it up. Where did that come from? Hmm. There was that burger before his flight last week. Could that have caused it? One burger? Although he had supersized the fries. Geez, and the drink. But that was just one meal. Mind you, his running shoes hadn't seen a road or a treadmill in a couple of months. Oh, and those beers and nachos while watching the Jays...

Your net worth is like your weight. Too many enchiladas and burgers and not enough exercise and you sprout a gut like David's. Switch to more nutritious options and a regular workout and muscles pop up, fat disappears and your belt becomes visible again. Each year the changes take you to a new state in your body composition. The same concept applies to your spending, saving and net worth.

Net worth is just the total of the things you own, minus what you owe. A positive net worth means your money works for you. It works while you are sleeping and while you are dining on ceviche on a patio. When your net worth is negative and debt-laden, it works against you, making you work harder just to keep up. It's like running up the down escalator: a whole lot of effort just to stay in the same place.

Let's go back to Bruno and make a net worth sheet, using the debts from his debt sheet on page 10.

Hmm. Lots of numbers. But they're not that hard to follow. The top section is things Bruno owns. His house and investments are going up in value over the years, which is great. Notice that the cars are dropping in value, which is why spending a lot on them is not great for your financial health.

The middle section is about what he owes. The mortgage is going down, as it should, but the credit cards are rising like a cake in a too-hot oven. Not good.

	2014	2015	2016
Things Bruno Has			
House	$586,500	$598,230	$610,195
RRSP	158,355	192,440	228,911
RESP	10,000	15,000	20,000
SUV	26,350	22,398	19,038
Car	18,700	15,895	13,511
Total assets	**$799,905**	**$843,962**	**$891,654**
What Bruno Owes			
Credit card 1	$3,700	$3,100	$3,700
Credit card 2	2,300	1,900	1,800
Car loan	25,000	17,000	11,000
Mortgage	371,000	357,000	347,000
Total debt	**$402,000**	**$379,000**	**$363,500**
Bruno's Net Worth	**$397,905**	**$464,962**	**$528,154**
Net Worth Change	**+$59,305**	**+$67,057**	**+$63,192**

The bottom part is very cool. In this case it shows that his net worth is rising and the bottom row shows how much it is changing each year. Having a positive and rising net worth means peace of mind. And options. Maybe financial freedom one day or the chance to start a business or pursue a more satisfying line of work that doesn't pay as well.

Where do you get the numbers? Cars and houses should be valued at what you could actually sell them for. For cars, check references like the Canadian Black Book or see what they're listed at on AutoTrader, Kijiji or Craigslist. Remember that prices in those types of ads are asking prices, not selling prices. Take off about 10% to be safe. For houses, see what similar ones have sold for in your neighbourhood. Don't include things like furniture, dishes and TVs in your assets. If you've ever tried to sell that stuff, you know their value is limited. The rest of the information you can get from your bank statements and wherever you have your debts and savings.

Take a moment now to set up a net worth sheet. Pull out your old records so you can go back at least two or three years. If technology isn't your thing, do it with a pen on the back of an envelope. Or beg a favour from your accountant friend to set one up. But get it done. Keep it somewhere safe and update it every three to six months to see how you are tracking.

If your net worth is negative you have some work to do and your focus needs to be on reducing debt. If your net worth is positive, but not really growing, you need to get off the "earn and burn treadmill" and get your money working for you.

If you have a positive and growing net worth, let's look for ways to speed up the process. In any case, the cashflow recipes in this book will be a big help.

Net Worth Tracking vs. Budgeting

One way to keep things on track is by managing expenditures to a budget, which can help keep your expenses at less than your income. This helps keep things in line for a period of time.

But a budget won't show you whether you are actually growing wealth. By tracking net worth as well, you can see if you are actually improving your overall financial health. Focusing on your net worth—seeing whether you're actually getting anywhere—will encourage you to continuously optimize your monthly expenditures to free up cashflow. This increased cashflow lets you pay down debt and buy more income-producing assets. The effects then compound as your wealth accelerates, creating options and peace of mind.

If you're only tracking to a budget, add the step of tracking net worth and focus on improving it each quarter and each year. You'll be glad you did.

When to Get Help

Some people may have genuine spending problems that need professional help. If you're stuck in the payday loan cycle, if creditors are calling, if you're losing sleep and your debts continue to grow, you may need credit counselling or other help with your attitudes about money and spending. Your financial concerns may require more help than you can get from a book. Put the book down and call someone.

How to Use the Recipes

With your debt sheet and your net worth sheet, you now have a sense of the state of your financial kitchen. If you have high-interest debts, you know that paying those off is top priority. If you have only low-interest mortgage debt, you will want to focus on building your wealth and getting your money working for you.

As you look through these recipes, you may feel the savings aren't realistic for you. Namaste. That's why there's a place for you to do your own math for each recipe. You may find that entire ideas don't apply to you. No problem. Flip ahead and taste the next recipe.

Important: As you work through the recipes, fire up the grill and immediately commit the savings to pay down debt or increase your savings. Set up or increase automated transfers right away. Don't just let the money stew in your chequing account. And don't rush to the mall with your newfound savings!

Here's how it can work:

Following her divorce, Vismaya wasn't sure how to make ends meet. Her deadbeat husband, Frank, wasn't making his support payments, and raising two daughters on her manager's salary wasn't easy. Vismaya spent some time studying her bank statements. The monthly cable bill stood out at $127. Vismaya never watched TV, and she didn't like it interfering with the girls' homework.

The high bill included sports packages that Frank had added; Vismaya felt pretty good about putting that on the chopping block.

   She called the cable company and cancelled her subscription, opting for a $11 Netflix subscription. This change freed up $116 each month. Vismaya immediately added that amount to her monthly car payment, allowing her to pay it off a year earlier, which, in turn, freed up another $340.

   With one simple change, Vismaya had made a dent in her debt and, with no cable TV there was actually some good conversation in the house. Unusual, but nice. She went back to her statements looking for more fat to trim.

Vismaya's case is pretty typical of the tasty rewards in this book: less time worrying about money, a financial cushion to cover unexpected expenses, your money growing and debts melting away. Sounds like a banquet of financial health!

   Just before we roll up our sleeves and start spattering ingredients around, a few more notes. Each recipe begins with some symbols:

$ More dollar signs mean more savings.

Y More whisks mean more effort to put the recipe into action.

⧗ An egg timer means the savings are longer term.

Each recipe includes suggested **ingredients**, but just like making soup, what you toss in the pot depends on your tastes and your circumstances. There's no reason to treat the recipes as cookie cutters.

   ☺ Some of the recipes include **Pro Chef Tips**.

   At the end of each recipe is a **yield table**. The example yields show you how much you would save if you invested your savings with a 7% return. Why 7%? It's a good long-term growth rate estimate for the stock market. It can also represent the cost of loans that you may want to pay down. If you want to use a different return, check the Utensils section of CashflowCookbook.com for a table of other future value factors and pick one that better reflects your situation.

To help you get started on serving up the savings, each recipe describes a **Light Serving**, showing the impact of the recipe on a single person or a small family, and **Hearty Serving**, which could apply to a larger family with more cars, houses, kids and stuff. These examples use some of the **ingredients** given for the recipe. They are there to show you a range of what the savings might look like.

Below the two example rows in the yield table is a row for **your info**. This is where you can do your own math to estimate your savings. Just plug in the numbers and follow the instructions. You will see what the recipe will be worth to you in savings each month, and the effect of those savings over 10 or 20 years. It's that easy!

Next is the **10-year value** column. Multiplying your monthly savings by 173 shows you what those savings will be worth over a 10-year period, assuming you invest the savings at 7% or pay down debt with that interest rate. The next column shows what the savings could be worth over **20 years** when compounded at 7%. To arrive at that value, multiply the monthly savings by 521.

Given the power of compounding, the savings become truly massive at 40 years, which sounds like an awfully long time. But if you're 25 and work until you're 65, that's 40 years. If you could use just one of the recipes that saves, say, $200 monthly, and you invested that money in the stock market and earned 7% over your 40-year career, you would have $524,800. Just from one recipe! Now that's tasty! To see how to do the 40-year math, visit the Utensils section of CashflowCookbook.com.

To complete your information, you may need to dig out some bills or bank statements. Remember, all the amounts are monthly, so if you have an annual number, just divide it by 12.

After you calculate your savings for each recipe you use, remember to adjust your monthly debt payments or automated savings by that amount.

Each section concludes with a **Take-Away Container**—the boiled-down essence of each recipe. Come back to these summaries in the years to come as your needs change.

Bon appétit!

Housing

HOUSING COSTS TAKE UP MORE than a quarter of the average Canadian household budget.[8] It's time to put them on a diet.

Some of these recipes will work if you are renting, but all of them can take a bite out of your expenses if you own a house or condo.

Every home expense presents an opportunity for savings, so let's get out the grater and start shaving them down to size. We will look at the costs of

- Utilities: gas and electricity
- Financing: mortgage costs
- Insurance: coverage and rates
- Contents: art, furniture, carpets, drapes, appliances
- Repairs: regular repairs and maintenance
- Alarms: it's not just the burglar ripping you off

And lots more.

Let's start with some of the easier recipes and work our way up to the advanced dishes.

---

[8] Statistics Canada, Average Household Spending by Province, Canada 2015.

Shish Kebabed Home Insurance $🍢🍢

With Bruno in his new, lower-paying job, he and Jodi increased their focus on household finances.

Jodi was leafing through her alumni magazine and noticed a home insurance ad that offered discounts to graduates. She pulled out their current policy and called the number in the ad.

Carefully comparing prices and coverage, she found a policy that offered identical protection but cost $250 less each year. Plus, the new company offered burglar alarm and smoke detector discounts that saved another $73.

Jodi's conversation took about 30 minutes, but will save $323 a year for years to come—that's good use of half an hour. She texted Bruno about her success and started wondering what other savings she could whip up.

By the time Bruno got home that night, Jodi had covered the dining room table with bank and credit card statements, looking to extend her savings buffet. While Jodi punched the calculator, Bruno quietly pocketed the credit card statements that included his new golf clubs and his last guys' trip to Vegas.

"I assume you grabbed those particular statements so you can look at ways to reduce your 'golf and guy' expenses," Jodi said without looking up.

Busted. Despite considerable effort, Bruno had no snappy comeback.

Coming home to a pile of uninsured ashes where your house used to stand certainly isn't fun. But having hundreds of dollars in insurance premiums singeing your chequing account each month isn't fun either.

Sure, finding savings on home insurance involves making a few calls, listening to some bad hold music and having to slowly spell your postal code to a robot several times. Be patient; it's worth it.

Put on your apron and start with your current insurer. Remember, they would rather keep you at a lower premium than lose you entirely. Call them up and ask them how best to lower your monthly costs. They'll do the work for you!

If you have a bit more time to spend in the kitchen, go online and check out other providers' rates for your city. You may find a great deal like Jodi did.

Ingredients

- Do some research, and call your existing company to optimize costs every few years.
- Don't over-insure—gather information on the actual value of your lot and contents and the cost of rebuilding your house.
- Aim for the highest deductible you can reasonably afford should you need to make a claim.
- Get quotes from multiple companies.
- Look at bundling home and car insurance with the same company.
- Take advantage of all possible discounts: home alarms, updated wiring, proximity to a fire hydrants, etc.
- Compare the total cost of paying monthly vs. annually—it can be 5% cheaper to pay annually.

- Never compromise coverage to save on premiums.
- Never leave your home uninsured while changing companies.
- Make sure you have adequate coverage for both building and contents.
- Check for coverage on things like flooding and vandalism.
- If you are renting, you still need contents insurance.

Hearty Serving

- Large home and a vacation property
- Insurance cost, $267 monthly
- Combined home and auto coverage, shopped to a new provider, aligned coverage with value of home and contents
- New insurance cost, $225 monthly

- Savings, $42 monthly

Light Serving
- One smaller home
- Insurance cost, $150 monthly
- Combined home and auto coverage, raised deductible, switched to annual payments from monthly
- New insurance cost, $117 monthly
- Savings, $33 monthly

Yield

Servings	Monthly Savings	10-Year Value × 173	20-Year Value × 521
Hearty	$42	$7,266	$21,882
Light	$33	$5,709	$17,193
Your info			

Imagine yourself, 20 years from now, wondering whether you should have invested an hour or two today to add $20,000 dollars or so to your net worth! Get these savings working right away by paying down debt or increasing your savings contributions.

Home Alarm Hash $ 🍸

With Frank moved out and the divorce final, Vismaya was starting to get things together, building her new life with their young daughters. Buoyed by the savings on the cable bill, she turned her attention to another of Frank's purchases: the home alarm system.

The tab was a shocking $60 a month, a lot more than what she heard advertised on the radio. It turns out that Frank had bought a top-of-the-line package that recorded video footage of anyone entering or leaving the house. As fascinating as it was to watch videos of her and her daughters coming and going, Vismaya valued the freed-up cash more.

Vismaya also realized she was paying $31 a month for a home phone line whose only purpose was to connect the alarm to the monitoring company. So the real cost, with the alarm and the phone line, was $91 monthly. She never used the landline phone, her daughters barely knew what it was for and the home alarm just needed a way to send a signal.

She switched to a more basic alarm plan and a cheaper wireless connection for the alarm. With the two changes, she saved $53 monthly. She used the freed-up cash to increase her RESP contributions for her daughters.

Being safe and secure in your home is as comforting as a big plate of shepherd's pie, but the cost of $35–$60 a month—or more—may leave a bad taste in your mouth.

Protecting your home is important (and, as Jodi learned, it can save on insurance premiums), but you may not need all the trimmings.

Let's cook up some savings! If you've had your system in place for some time, you are likely now "out of contract," meaning you own the actual alarm gear and are free to move the monitoring of the system to a lower-cost provider.

No home alarm? Just move on to the next recipe.

Ingredients

- Review your current alarm contract or call your provider to see if you are still under contract.
- Research discount alarm monitoring companies in your area. How many years in business? Any Better Business Bureau complaints? Online reviews? Are they compatible with your existing alarm hardware?
- Ask your existing company and some of the discount monitoring firms for their best quotes.
- Go bake your best deal!

> Be sure you have coverage during company changeover and make sure the new system is thoroughly tested.

Hearty Serving

- Two properties
- Two monitored alarms at $40 = $80 monthly
- Switched to discount monitoring at $10 monthly each
- New cost, $20 monthly
- Savings, $60 monthly

Light Serving

- One home
- Monitored alarm costing $32 monthly
- Switched to discount monitoring at $10 monthly
- New cost, $10
- Savings, $22 monthly

Yield

Servings	Monthly Savings	10-Year Value × 173	20-Year Value × 521
Hearty	$60	$10,380	$31,260
Light	$22	$3,806	$11,462
Your info			

Add your data to the table above, lock the freed-up cash into debt reduction or increased savings and you are on to the next recipe. Keep track of your total savings as you complete each recipe.

Glazed Snow Removal with a Side of Frozen Fingerlings

Bruno glanced out the window while getting breakfast organized. The snow was spewing down. Major roads were open, as were schools, but there was a good 15 cm of snow on the driveway and his car certainly wouldn't make it out. Of course, the plowing service he had hired for the season was jammed with work and hadn't yet made it to his driveway.

Bruno had an 8:30 AM meeting. He called his neighbour, Steve, to mooch a ride with him in his all-wheel drive truck. Steve griped about the same problem with his snow removal service. They never arrived early enough, their plow had clipped his air conditioner unit one year and had knocked out a couple of Bruno's automatic lawn sprinkler heads another year.

As they drove to work, they hatched a plan to take matters into their own cold hands. They would split the cost of a used snow blower and take turns doing the clearing. It might mean three mornings each of getting up early but the cost savings, convenience and autonomy would be well worth it.

In the spring, Steve got a great deal on a snow blower from a work friend who was being transferred to Bermuda and had limited need of the machine there. Steve brought it home in his truck and he and Bruno spent a couple of hours changing the engine oil, greasing the bearings and pumping the tires to the correct pressure. Bruno found a can of tire soap and a rag and brought the tires up to a rich black sheen. Steve dressed up the discharge chute with a couple of car racing stickers. The guy time was interrupted as their wives arrived to survey the final aesthetic efforts.

"Um, just wrapping up," offered Bruno, glancing up at the women.

"Should be able to save us about $300 a year each—we can put it toward the kids' education," suggested Steve, quickly grabbing a wrench and feigning an adjustment.

If you have a snow removal service coming to your home to clear your driveway and sidewalk, you may be blowing cash as well as snow.

Plowing services face a challenge: the heavier the snowfall, the busier their day, which means on the days you most need them, they're often late digging you out. That's about as useful as stirring the chili *after* it's a burnt mass welded to the bottom of the pot.

Let's chop some excess costs.

Ingredients

- If you don't have much of a driveway, let me put this gently: Set down the remote and if you are able, rise up from the couch and do some shovelling!

- Too lazy? Not able? Find a dependable local teenager to do it. Perhaps you raised one yourself and it is time for them to get to work!

- If you have a disability or are over 65, you may be eligible for free snow removal service. Check with your municipality.

- Check out the new Uber-like on-demand snow removal apps such as SnowMowr, Easyplow and Eden on Google Play and the Apple App Store—see if their rates are better than the seasonal contracted guys.

- If you have a big driveway, why not find a neighbour and go halves on a used snow blower? Odd days of the month, you do the work, even days, she covers it.

  - Shop on Kijiji or Craigslist for used snow blowers. Check for clean oil on the dipstick. Does the machine look like it's been cared for? Start it up and give it a test drive. If you need to, take a mechanically minded friend to give it the once over. Do your shopping in the spring for the best deals on new and used blowers.

  - Do your own maintenance. With the owner's manual and a bit of YouTube research, you can learn to change the oil and spark plug and do a bit of seasonal greasing. Or at least watch a knowledgeable neighbour handle it.

Hearty Serving

- Two neighbouring households with large driveways
- Each paying equivalent of $67 monthly for snow plowing
- Split the cost of a large used snow blower, $600 each
- New cost over 48-month lifespan, $6.25 monthly; call it $7 monthly including some do-it-yourself maintenance
- Savings, $60 monthly

Light Serving

- Two neighbouring households with small driveways
- Each paying equivalent of $33 monthly for snow plowing
- Split the cost of a small used snow blower, $400 each
- New cost over 48-month lifespan, $4.16 monthly; call it $5 monthly including some do-it-yourself maintenance
- Savings, $29 monthly

Yield

Servings	Monthly Savings	10-Year Value × 173	20-Year Value × 521
Hearty	$60	$10,380	$31,260
Light	$29	$5,017	$15,109
Your info			

Great savings, fresh air, exercise and self-sufficiency. And only you and your neighbour to blame if the job isn't done on time! Yes, it works for grass cutting too!

Gas Bill Gumbo $ $ ♟ ♟

Brad and Lucy had lived in the same house for more than 30 years. Their son, Stan, had returned home after completing his music degree and had taken up residence in their basement, where he conducted his piano lesson business.

In addition to their new hobby of listening to loud, discordant music, Brad and Lucy tried to keep busy while managing their finances through their retirement with their savings and small government pension. They had closed their travel agency business when online bookings became the norm. Finances were tight.

Three years ago, they had hired Frank the contractor to relocate their laundry facilities up to the main floor. It saved them the stair climb and left more room in the basement for Stan. The new setup was great, but for some reason, the new laundry room was awfully cold in the winter, and the house had developed a musty smell.

Brad finally investigated and discovered that the dryer vent had never been properly connected, leaving them with a four-inch hole to the outside behind the dryer and a lot of moist laundry air in the house. Brad pondered the cost of the extra heating he had been paying for the past few years and started a mission to properly seal the house. He began with the dryer vent and then upgraded weather stripping and caulked some gaps. He looked for air leaks by noting smoke movement as he held a stick of lit incense near door and window frames, electrical outlets and wall-mounted light fixtures.

Lucy found him wandering around the house in his boxer shorts, undershirt, black dress socks and reading glasses waving a stick of watermelon incense. She drew a breath to speak, but then reasoned that after 40 years of marriage, sometimes it's best not to ask questions.

Brad's "tour de incense," however, paid off with a $300 reduction in the annual gas bill.

What's more fun than paying the gas bill? Anything. Everything.

The average Canadian gas heating bill is about $150 monthly. In larger or less-efficient homes, the bills can easily be double that. So the savings are no small potatoes.

Gas rates are not negotiable, so a few phone calls and a silver tongue won't help on this one. Instead, the savings come from simple home adjustments and a bit of handiwork. Learn some DIY skills, recruit a handy friend or pay a local tradesperson to get it done.

Ingredients

- Consider a home energy audit to map out the highest-return projects. A few hundred dollars can bake a plan for years of savings. Look for a reputable contractor and check online reviews. Check with your municipality or province to see if there are grants available to cover some or all of the costs.
- Set-back and programmable thermostats can lower gas costs in the winter by 10% by reducing nighttime and away-from-home heating costs. The ones that connect to wi-fi even have apps that let you control your heating and cooling remotely. Cool. Or warm.
- Better door and window weather stripping can save 10%.
- Improved attic insulation can save another 10%.
- Keeping furnace filters clean can save 5%.
- If you heat your hot water with gas, consider switching from baths to showers.
- Replace your showerheads with low-flow models.
- Use the cold-water setting on your washing machine (remember to get the cold-water detergent).
- Upgraded windows and doors can provide savings too, so look at high-efficiency products when it's time to replace them. Any windows with a broken seal (you will see moisture between the double panes) have lost most of their energy efficiency and should be replaced or repaired right away.
- High-efficiency furnaces are generally worth the incremental costs—this can be assessed during your energy audit, but if it's time to replace the unit get a high-efficiency model.

> If your house or hot water are heated by electricity or propane rather than natural gas, all of these tips will still save you money.

Hearty Serving
- Two properties
- Total gas bill of $317 monthly
- Installed two set-back thermostats to save $32 monthly
- Replaced old weather stripping, sealed air gaps to save $32 monthly
- Improved attic insulation in both homes to save $32 monthly
- Inspected/replaced furnace filters every two months to save $7 monthly (net of filter cost)
- Savings, $103 monthly

Light Serving
- Small house
- Gas bill of $125 monthly
- Installed set-back thermostat to save $12 monthly
- Replaced old weather stripping, sealed air gaps to save $13 monthly
- Improved attic insulation to save $13 monthly
- Inspected/replaced furnace filters every two months to save $4 monthly (net of filter costs)
- Savings, $42 monthly

Yield

Servings	Monthly Savings	10-Year Value × 173	20-Year Value × 521
Hearty	$103	$17,819	$53,663
Light	$42	$7,266	$21,882
Your info			

These savings amounts and percentages are approximate, given the country's various climates, the wide variety of homes, their condition and the level of improvement required. Keep in mind that some winters are milder than others so you should look at your spending over a two- or three-year period. Also, some of these ideas may require some investment, which may be deducted as a one-time cost from the 10- and 20-year total savings in the yield table.

Electric Bill Braised in a
Juice Reduction

$ $ ♟ ♟

Vismaya was putting out her trash early one Wednesday morning. While rolling her garbage and recycling bins out of the garage, she banged her elbow on her ex-husband's beer fridge. Once the pain subsided, she resumed her trips to the curb, but then came back and looked at the fridge. She opened the door to see seven beers inside, the fridge labouring in the August heat to keep them cold. Vismaya hadn't had a beer since university.

She unplugged the fridge and left the beers at the curb in a neat box with a sign for the garbage crew. As she closed the garage door, she heard the rumble of the truck and looked back to see the garbage guy hanging onto the truck with one hand and drinking an ice-cold breakfast beer with the other. The driver was also tipping a cold one. Vismaya's mom instincts kicked in and she sprinted after the truck in her slippers, pyjamas and housecoat. The truck came to a stop. The workers were laughing.

As Vismaya got closer she realized the caps were still on the beers.

"Thanks," the driver said. "But we'll save them for after the shift."

Vismaya walked back to her house smiling and shaking her head, her housecoat belt dragging behind her.

She did some searching online and found out that her municipality took old fridges away at no cost. The next week, her fridge was gone, as was more than $20 a month on her electricity bill. Vismaya immediately increased her automated monthly TFSA savings contributions by $20.

The average Canadian household spends about $150 a month for 1,000 kWh. As with the gas bill, there's no joy in sending your cash to the electric company and no amount of whining will make them reduce your bill. But there are opportunities to reduce the juice.

Ingredients

- Exorcise that phantom power. Your plugged-in computers, stereos and other gadgets can suck over $200 a year from your bank account even when they are off. Spooky. Get yourself some smart power bars or unplug the unused toys.

- Reduce the air conditioner use. A smart set-back thermostat can cool your home only when you need it. Try settings that are slightly warmer than your norm. Can you set it one degree warmer and still be comfortable? An air-conditioned house doesn't have to feel like a meat locker. Consider installing window film to reflect heat.

- If your older furnace/air conditioner fan is set to run continuously, consider changing the fan setting on your thermostat to "auto" from "on." This will allow the fan to run only when needed.

- Switch to LED lightbulbs. They use one-fifth the power of incandescent bulbs. And no, the light doesn't look strange if you get the right bulbs. Buy "warm white" for most rooms and "daylight" for garages, work rooms and laundry rooms. Note that the cost and power consumption of LED bulbs continue to drop, making them a better and better idea.

- Run the dryer and dishwasher in off-peak hours; low rates are about half as much as high rates in time-of-use billing areas. Many dishwashers have a delay feature for this purpose. Bonus: you don't have to listen to your dishwasher if it runs while you sleep.

- Consider one of those new solar powered clothes dryers, also known as clotheslines. Fresh-smelling clothes, easy on the environment and a big reduction to your electric bill.

- Your mother was right: putting on a sweater is way cheaper than putting on a heater. Those juice hogs can cost 60 bucks a month!

- Lose that old beer fridge. It's cracking open an extra $20 a month.

- Use a pool cover to reduce heater costs, which can be as high as $400 a month.

And of course, simply turning things off when you're not using them is always helpful, though it runs contrary to the approach of most teenagers. And some spouses.

> If you live in an apartment with baseboard or radiator heat and it tends to be dry in the winter, consider washing your clothes and hanging them in your apartment to dry. Doing so saves on dryer costs and planetary resources while adding needed moisture to your air.

Hearty Serving
- Two properties
- Total electricity bill of $333 monthly
- Reduced air conditioner use to save $17 monthly
- Unplugged and removed rarely used second fridge to save $20 monthly
- Installed swimming pool cover when not in use to save $67 monthly
- Replaced 20 most-used lightbulbs with LEDs to save $20 monthly
- Began using appliances during lower-priced billing times to save $17 monthly
- Savings, $140 monthly

Light Serving
- Small house
- Electricity bill of $150 monthly
- Reduced air conditioner use to save $10 monthly
- Switched furnace fan to "auto" from "on" to save $18 monthly
- Replaced 10 most-used lightbulbs with LEDs to save $10 monthly

- Reduced use of portable electric heaters to save $12 monthly
- Began using appliances during lower-priced billing times to save $8 monthly
- Savings, $58 monthly

Yield

Servings	Monthly Savings	10-Year Value × 173	20-Year Value × 521
Hearty	$140	$24,220	$72,940
Light	$58	$10,034	$30,218
Your info			

There are dozens of ways to take the brûlée torch to your electricity bill with minimal investment and effort. Experiment and look at your annual power summary on your bill to check on your progress. Lock the savings away in debt reduction or investments.

Home Furnishing Fricassee $ $ 🍴 🍴

Bruno and Jodi's younger son, Thomas, was interested in music and had started taking piano lessons. His cheap electronic keyboard wasn't the ideal practice machine and a few trips to piano stores revealed that even a basic piano would cost several thousand dollars. Sadly, finances were tight and a new piano wasn't in the budget. They decided they would have to do without.

One Saturday morning, they noticed a carefully drawn picture of a piano that Thomas had created and taped to the fridge. Bruno and Jodi looked sadly at each other. They knew what they had to do.

They settled on a new piano from the music store. With tax, the total was just under $4,520. Luckily, the store manager approved them for financing at 18% over four years. Bruno glanced briefly at the interest rate and the total interest cost of $1,856, but, well, family first. And after all, the payments were only $132.84 a month.

Thomas was thrilled.

When Bruno picked up Thomas from his lesson with Stan, the two men talked pianos. Bruno asked about the beautiful one that Thomas used at his lessons. And grimaced with actual physical pain when Stan said he got it from the free section of Kijiji.

"I never pay for pianos. They're big and heavy and people need them gone before the movers show up. Take a piano teacher for the inspection and hire a piano mover. It's a major score!" said Stan cheerily.

It was a quiet ride home for Bruno and Thomas.

Ever try to sell home furnishings you no longer want? They're about as appealing to other people as last month's leftovers, and just as challenging to sell. With luck, you might get 10 cents on the dollar.

But turn that idea around the other way. Why not shop for all your home furnishings and accessories this way? The bigger and bulkier the item, the better the deal to be had. Check the free section of Craigslist and Kijiji: I bet there are several working appliances and couches in there that need to be taken away by Friday. Just about everything else can be found at a discount from new in the paid sections.

Ingredients
- For large or heavy things, use local sites like Craigslist and Kijiji.
- For lighter things that can be shipped, extend your search to eBay.
- Have a look at FreeCycle.org as a way of donating or receiving free things.
- Set up alerts on Kijiji so you get an email when the thing you want becomes available. Very cool. Bargain hunting, but without the hunting.
- Check out garage and estate sales and let your friends know what you are looking for.
- Be patient. If you are willing to wait a bit, you can get what you need for a fraction of the price of a new one.

What's out there? You name it! From carpets to couches, lighting to dining room sets, someone is selling it, even full sets of kitchen cabinets and beautiful artwork. For outdoors, there is high-end patio furniture, trampolines and fire pits. Do some searching and get inspired!

> Be alert for bed bugs before bringing anything home.
> Don't buy used mattresses—get new ones on sale.

Hearty Serving
- One home and one vacation property
- Saved $167 monthly on average on home furnishings
- Examples: dining room set, or a few pieces of art and a living room carpet in a year
- Savings, $167 monthly

Light Serving

- One home
- Saved $83 monthly on average on home furnishings
- Examples: a set of bar stools and a coffee table, or a couch and some side chairs in a year
- Savings, $83 monthly

Yield

Servings	Monthly Savings	10-Year Value × 173	20-Year Value × 521
Hearty	$167	$28,891	$87,007
Light	$83	$14,359	$43,243
Your info			

Instead of feeling desperate to get that new couch or coffee table this weekend, relax and enjoy the hunt for the perfect bargain piece! You've heard of the slow food movement? Think of this as slow furniture.

Marinated Mortgage Rate on Rye

$ $ 🌶 ⚱ ⚱ ⚱

Stan the piano teacher and his partner Richard were in cramped quarters living in Stan's parents' basement, which did double duty as a piano studio. So when Stan's aunt passed away and left him an inheritance, a home of their own was a priority. It was a tight market, but they were thrilled when their offer was accepted on a small brick bungalow. They didn't fully think through the implications of the railway tracks nearby, but that's another story.

Stan shared the great news with his bank manager, who wasted no time drawing up the mortgage papers. Later that week when Bruno came to pick up his son, Thomas, from his piano lesson, Stan excitedly told Bruno about the new home and the upcoming relocation of the lessons. Bruno asked where Stan was getting the financing and suggested that he let him provide a mortgage quote, given that he worked at a credit union. At first Stan protested, since he had a close relationship with his banker.

In the end, Bruno provided a rate that Stan's banker could not match. The new rate saved Stan and Richard over $200 a month. Wisely, they kept the payments at the original higher level, saving years of mortgage payments and thousands of dollars of interest.

Even if your chequing account, savings account, credit cards and investments are all at one bank, don't feel compelled to get your mortgage there too. It's not a supermarket.

Mortgage rates can vary a lot and getting the best rate makes a big difference, freeing up cash to pay off higher-interest debt or to just get rid of the mortgage faster.

Ingredients

- Do some web shopping for rates at the major banks.
- Extend your search to smaller banks and credit unions.
- Connect with a licensed mortgage broker to see their options.

- In addition to the rate, be sure to compare
  - Terms and conditions
  - Fees and penalties
  - Extra payment and prepayment options
  - Pre-approvals
  - Portability, renewal rates and other features
  - Stability of the lender

> If you already have a mortgage, but the rate is higher than the current market rate, ask your bank if you can open a home equity line of credit (HELOC) at a lower rate and use it to prepay a portion of your mortgage (often mortgages will allow a 15% prepayment). This works well if the HELOC rate is significantly lower than your existing mortgage rate, and if you have generous annual prepayment options (10–15%). You can continue this approach each year, assuming the HELOC rate remains below your mortgage rate.
>
> The other option, if you are locked into a higher-than-market mortgage, is to break the mortgage, but banks usually charge an interest rate differential (IRD) that negates the benefit of breaking the mortgage. But check.

Shopping for mortgages is a bit like selecting fruit at a grocery store. You shouldn't buy the first cantaloupe you see. You need to do a good deal of sniffing, squeezing and tapping before making a selection.

In the examples below, we will use 10-year closed mortgages with a 20-year amortization. A rate reduction saves on both monthly payments and total interest paid.

Hearty Serving
- $500,000 mortgage

- 6.1% interest over 10 years = $253,716; over 20 years = $361,657
- Monthly payment, $3,589
- Got rate reduced from 6.1% to 5.35%
- 5.35% interest over 10 years = $220,218; over 20 years = $311,602
- New monthly payment, $3,381
- Interest savings: 10-year = $33,498; 20-year = $50,055
- Savings, $208 monthly

Light Serving
- $250,000 mortgage
- 6.1% interest over 10 years = $126,858; over 20 years = $180,129
- Monthly payment, $1,794
- Got rate reduced from 6.1% to 5.85%
- 5.85% interest over 10 years = $121,256; over 20 years = $172,406
- New monthly payment, $1,759
- Interest savings: 10-year = $5,602; 20-year = $7,723
- Savings, $35 monthly

Yield

Servings	Monthly Savings	10-Year Value × 173 + Interest Savings	20-Year Value × 521 + Interest Savings
Hearty	$208	$69,482	$158,423
Light	$35	$11,657	$25,958
Your info			

The total savings include both the value of the monthly payment savings and the total interest saved over the 10 or 20 years. Your financial institution can give you these numbers or you can use an online bank mortgage calculator.

If you are uncomfortable doing the shopping yourself, get a quote or two from the bank and then connect with a licensed mortgage broker. These kinds of savings justify the larger effort.

Mortgage Life Insurance Mousse $ $ ¥

Vismaya was starting to make some headway on her finances. The divorce from Frank was tough but she was rebuilding her life and working to set up her daughters for their future.

In January, the annual mortgage summary came and Vismaya gave it a once over. She knew it was a slow process to pay off a mortgage and she had other priorities in the meantime. She was about to file the statement when she noticed the section about mortgage life insurance.

She knew the mortgage was insured by a bank policy that would pay off the mortgage if she died. The idea of the protection was good, but she noticed that the cost of the insurance was over $110 a month and was blended in with the mortgage payment.

Vismaya did some online research and was able to get a term life policy for about $45 a month that would cover more than triple the amount of her mortgage. In addition, the term life policy would protect her for the full amount, while the mortgage life insurance covered only the value of the mortgage, which declined each year.

She could get much better protection for her daughters—and save $65 per month. She signed up for the new policy, made sure it was in force and then removed the mortgage life insurance and increased her mortgage payments by the $65 she saved each month. By upping her payments she would be able to save on interest and pay her house off sooner, all with no sacrifice.

OK, now we are into the sweet stuff. Who doesn't get an appetite when we are tossing around tasty words like "mortgage" and "life insurance"?

Insurance is there to protect your dependents financially if something happens to you, the one with the income. So having enough insurance is a good idea.

How you do that protecting is another story. Get help from a licensed insurance broker to find out how much coverage you need, or use one of the calculators on bank and insurance company web-sites. Once you know how much you need, buy the coverage the right way.

There are a few problems with mortgage life insurance:

- It costs three or four times as much as level term insurance (which allows you to pay the same premiums throughout the term of the insurance, usually 10 or 20 years).
- You continue to pay the same premium, even though your mortgage shrinks each month. So in your first month you are paying, say, three times too much.
- In your last month, you have almost no mortgage to insure and you are paying the same as you did when you first got your mortgage. So you are paying, like, infinity times too much.
- Unlike regular term life insurance, mortgage life insurance is not always guaranteed to pay out because the insurer doesn't verify your health status before signing the policy. So you risk being denied payment if the insurance company determines, after your death, that they won't pay out due to some sort of pre-existing condition.
- Yes, that is completely crazy.

Ingredients

- Check your total insurance needs versus how much coverage you have.
- If you already have enough coverage and don't need the mortgage life insurance, cancel it or don't buy it in the first place.
- If you do need more coverage, buy additional term life insurance and then cancel or don't buy the mortgage insurance.

Hearty Serving

- 41-year-old male non-smoker
- $500,000 of mortgage life insurance at $220 monthly
- Confirmed he has adequate coverage with other policies
- Cancelled mortgage life insurance
- Savings, $220 monthly

Light Serving

- 41-year-old female non-smoker
- $250,000 of mortgage life insurance at $110 monthly
- Added $250,000 of 20-year term life insurance at $26 monthly
- Cancelled mortgage life insurance
- Saving, $84 monthly

Yield

Servings	Monthly Savings	10-Year Value × 173	20-Year Value × 521
Hearty	$220	$38,060	$114,620
Light	$84	$14,532	$43,764
Your info			

Wow! Don't waste any of those savings. Spoon them straight into your debts, or use them to garnish your registered savings plans.

Home Repair Ratatouille $ $ 🍴 🍴

Stan and Richard were settling into their new home. Most things worked well, but there were a few issues, like the stove that wouldn't light properly in three of the four burners. It was an older gas model that had come with the house and replacing it was just not in the budget right now. Using a lighter to get it going might lead to some singed eyebrows, or worse, so Stan booked an appointment with a repair service, agreeing to the $100 service fee and a $100/hour labour charge, plus parts.

Stan let the repair technician in and showed him the problem. The tech nodded sagely and asked for a paperclip. Stan was a bit puzzled but produced one. The tech straightened it out, removed the burner covers and poked around in the gas jet hole, then blew the debris out. He tested the burners, which all ignited flawlessly, and wrote up a bill for $200 plus tax.

"$200 to poke the debris from those little holes?! I could have done that myself," gasped Stan.

"Yes, but you didn't." The repair guy winked. "You're lucky you had your own paperclip. Usually I have to charge for those!" Kindly, he handed Stan back his straightened paperclip.

After the tech left, Stan did some searching on YouTube and found a number of videos showing the paperclip trick. Intrigued, he searched around and found hundreds of home repair videos covering everything from icemaker fixes to tile installation and humidifier maintenance. Stan vowed to start any future home projects with a trip to YouTube University.

Enough with the expensive repairs that pack a punch like a Szechuan hotpot. Before calling a pro, consider some home remedies.

Ingredients

- Recruit some help from a talented handy friend. Get the current job done and learn how to do it yourself for next time.
- Spend some time on YouTube. Search for any home fix-it job and let people with experience show you how it's done.

- Search on home fix-it websites such as RepairClinic.com, HowStuffWorks.com or DoItYourself.com.
- Check your local building supply stores for free seminars on home repair techniques.
- Do an internet search for local building codes to ensure your work is being done safely.

- Always use appropriate safety gear, including safety glasses, hearing protection, dust masks and whatnot.
- Don't attempt a repair that is beyond your capabilities.
- Always follow local codes and inspection protocols and get necessary permits.
- If in doubt, call a professional.

Start with the mundane, like learning how to clean eaves troughs, change furnace filters and replace door handles. Then, if you are getting into it, move to some small projects like installing a light fixture, unclogging a drain, painting a room or replacing a faucet. Still enjoying the DIY? Work your way up to installing ceramic tiling, fixing a washing machine or installing shelving.

Hearty Serving

- One home and one vacation property
- Saved the labour cost on $250 in projects on average monthly
- Examples: replacing boards on a deck, replacing a refrigerator icemaker or painting some rooms
- Savings, $250 monthly

Light Serving

- One home
- Saved the labour cost on $83 in projects on average monthly
- Examples: clearing drains a couple of times, installing shelving and replacing a broken faucet
- Savings, $83 monthly

Yield

Servings	Monthly Savings	10-Year Value × 173	20-Year Value × 521
Hearty	$250	$43,250	$130,250
Light	$83	$14,359	$43,243
Your info			

Great savings, plus the satisfaction of doing the work yourself.

Self-Storage Sashimi

$ $ 🍴 🍴

Vismaya had made good progress on her finances, but she continued to look for opportunities to improve. In studying her bank statements, she took a second look at a monthly storage locker fee of $163. The locker held some of her ex-husband's old construction gear. As far as she could recall, it didn't even contain any of her things. Frank had originally sent her to rent it for him, so the locker was in her name.

Vismaya called Frank and told him he had until Friday to take what he needed from the locker. On Saturday, Vismaya opened the air-conditioned locker and found a collection of home repair tools and, strangely, a case of Malbec. She gave the tools to a handy friend in exchange for labour on future home repairs.

She cancelled the locker and immediately added $163 to her monthly credit card payment, which would allow her to pay it off in 10 months. She would then add that amount to her mortgage payments.

When she got home, she remembered her daughters were at a sleepover. She smiled to herself, pulled a murder mystery from the bookshelf, opened a bottle of the Malbec, poured a glass and admired the smooth mouth feel and notes of blackberry, dark chocolate and leather while fantasizing that the murder victim was her ex.

Ever get the sense that you own too much crap? Maybe it's the garage you can't get your car in, the basement you can't walk through or the closets that drop objects on you when you open them. Do you get tired just looking at it all?

Do you have a storage locker fee that's squeezing your budget like a lemon?

Embark on a big purge of the junk you don't need. What should you get rid of?

Ingredients

- Things your kids have outgrown, and no, don't save stuff for grandchildren. Buy gently used replacement gear for them if and when they arrive.
- Anything you haven't touched in more than two years, and that includes the boxes that contain you-know-not-what.
- Broken things. Get them fixed or sold or thrown out.
- Stuff you are storing for offspring who have grown and moved away. Send it to them.
- Boxes of clothing you haven't worn in years. Ladies, that includes your 1980s power suits with the CFL shoulder pads and gents, those oversized suits with the high waists and pleated pants are just begging to be donated or altered to a more modern state by a gifted tailor.
- Furniture that doesn't work with your current home. It's unlikely to work with your next home either.
- Documents, including tax records older than the required six-year holding period.

Organizing guru Marie Kondo talks about keeping only things that give you joy. Great concept. There is limited joy available from your broken vacuum cleaner. It's also tough to find it in your kids' old playpen, complete with dried spit-up on the rails. Especially now that they're in university.

Be ruthless. Get everything you don't need into a big pile. It's time for a yard sale, some online listings or a helpful donation. Some charities will even come and pick it up. Things you keep will need some shelving or cabinets to free up space. Your home can now store the things that bring you joy. The cash goes into your TFSA where it can generate some financial joy.

And now you can eliminate or downsize your storage locker. Do some math on the actual value of what you are storing there. If you couldn't sell it all for $1,000, does it make sense to pay hundreds a month to store it?

Hearty Serving
- Large, climate-controlled storage locker
- Locker rental fee, $450 monthly
- Eliminated need for locker entirely
- Savings, $450 monthly

Light Serving
- Medium-sized locker
- Locker rental fee, $250 monthly
- Downsized to small locker for $150 monthly
- Savings, $100 monthly

Yield

Servings	Monthly Savings	10-Year Value × 173	20-Year Value × 521
Hearty	$450	$77,850	$234,450
Light	$100	$17,300	$52,100
Your info			

Incredible. Nearly a quarter of a million dollars over 20 years to store stuff you will likely throw out when you retire—or that your heirs will relegate to a Dumpster when you die.

The Take-Away Container

In this section, we looked at 10 areas that can earn a potential $104,039 for our Light Serving and $327,598 for the Hearty Serving over 10 years when invested at 7%:

✓ **Dare to compare.** Check for proper insurance coverage, combine home and car insurance, shop around for the best rate.

✓ **Smart home protection.** Discount home alarm companies can be a low-calorie alternative.

✓ **Grab a shovel.** Consider splitting a snow blower, and snow clearing duty, with a neighbour.

✓ **Stop wasting heat.** Install programmable thermostats, clean furnace filters, improved weather stripping and attic insulation.

✓ **Find the electricity wasters.** Install LED lighting, remove extra refrigerators and cut power to unused electronics.

✓ **Furnish some savings.** Shop online for used furnishings.

✓ **Manage the mortgage.** Shop aggressively for the best mortgage and terms and use a HELOC to tenderize a high-rate mortgage.

✓ **Lose the mortgage life insurance.** Check your mortgage needs and replace expensive, uncertain mortgage life insurance with term coverage.

✓ **Fix it yourself.** Sharpen your basic home repair skills with YouTube videos and books.

✓ **Empty the locker.** Estimate the value of what you are storing compared with its monthly storage cost. Get rid of stuff you don't need.

Continuously look at your recurring housing costs to find ways to improve. Check out the Ingredients section at CashFlowCookbook.com for tested products and services that can help.

Cars & Transportation

TRANSPORTATION COSTS CONSUME more than 20% of the average Canadian household budget. It's enough to drive your finances into the ditch.

Next up is a set of recipes to grill those costs one by one. Car expenses are easy to miss—a half tank of gas here, a car wash there and $20 for parking. Not a big deal...

Until you add everything up at the end of the month. A brand-new, leased SUV can easily cost more than $1,600 per month, including payments, gas, maintenance, parking and insurance. Even an economy car can still run $415 per month.

Here are the basics for some significant savings:

- — Buy a gently used but well-maintained vehicle, ideally with some warranty coverage left.
- — Keep your vehicle for several years.
- — Buy brands with a history of reliability.
- — Get a vehicle that meets your needs 95% of the time.
- — Learn eco-driving techniques.
- — Combine trips.
- — Drive less by walking, biking, taking transit, carpooling.
- — Avoid buying cars that must run on premium fuel.

Those are just the appetizers; let's break out the Ginsu knives to do some transportation cost chopping.

Traffic-Beating Beets $ ¶

Frank was having a rough morning. There was trouble with one of his renovation projects. It was going poorly and the homeowner was threatening to sue because of cost and time overruns. Frank had agreed to meet with the homeowner as well as the supervisors of each of his trades at the jobsite at 9 AM.

It was Frank's week with his daughters and he wasn't as good as his ex-wife at getting the kids organized and off to school. By the time he had their lunches packed, the girls were worried about being late for school.

In the flurry of activity, Frank lost track of time. He finally got the girls in the truck and glanced at the clock. 8:41. Ugh.

He dropped the girls at school. 8:53. They would need notes from the principal's office to get into class. Frank would need more than a note to save him from his client.

It would take about 20 minutes to get to the jobsite. Frank called the homeowner and let him know he would be there for 9:20. Frank took the expressway because the adjacent road looked slow. Five minutes later, the expressway was at a standstill behind a massive accident. Frank looked over at the road to see the cars speeding along.

He arrived at the jobsite at 9:50 to face an angry homeowner and disgruntled trades. The meeting was cancelled, the trades walked off and the homeowner was unwilling to pay for the work to date.

On the bright side, he would be on time for the girls' piano recital that night.

Cars are expensive, which is why we have a car section. And they are expensive whether they are moving or not. But if you could prune, say, 5% of your gas and repairs by shortening either total drive time or distance, that adds up to real savings. Delicious!

Waze is a free app that optimizes your route by knowing the speed limits, the speed of every other Waze user on every route and the info that friendly Wazers provide to the app, such as speed traps, accidents and construction delays. Follow Waze for the best route and save a good 5% on reduced driving time, gas, mileage, wear and tear and repairs.

As a bonus, you can end arguments with yourself or your spouse as to which route is the best. Let the all-seeing, all-knowing app optimize your routing. Find something new to argue about!

You can actually see it working when the app reroutes you onto some concession road you have never heard of after you see one-third of the drivers ahead take the same unspoken digital detour. The rest of the "suckahs" head, unknowing, straight into the jam.

Ingredients

- Download the free Waze app, or a similar real-time traffic app, to your smartphone.
- Let the app do the navigating and enjoy a fully optimized route every time.
- Save on gas, maintenance, arguments and time.

Beet the traffic. Beet the costs. Beet wasted time. Sorry; couldn't resist.

- Get one of those nifty clamps for your phone that attaches to a vent or the CD player in your car. Saves you holding it while you drive (illegal) or trying to catch it as it slides across your dashboard or falls under your seat (likely worse).
- Turn on the turn-by-turn voice instructions so you don't need to look at the screen.
- No peeking at your email, stock prices or Facebook feeds with your phone perched up there. Stay focused on your driving.

Hearty Serving

- Two cars
- Total of $600 in gas + $300 in repairs = $900 of monthly expenses
- Saved 5% through reduced car use using optimized routing

- Savings, $45 monthly

Light Serving
- One car
- $200 in gas + $50 in repairs = $250 of monthly expenses
- Saved 5% through reduced car use using optimized routing
- Savings, $12 monthly

Yield

Servings	Monthly Savings	10-Year Value × 173	20-Year Value × 521
Hearty	$45	$7,785	$23,445
Light	$12	$2,076	$6,252
Your info			

Not bad for a free app! The savings are tasty and arriving on time is just the glaze on the beets. Help other Wazers by noting accidents, slowdowns and potholes (but only after you park, or if you're the passenger). Use the savings to chop your debts!

Car Wash Clafouti

$ 🏆

When Bruno worked at the bank, he would drive to work each day and park underneath the bank's office tower. He loved that he could walk from his house to his attached garage, drive to his underground spot at the bank and take the elevator right up to his office. Very pleasing to do the whole trip without freezing or getting wet.

His car, however, did get wet and dirty. Bruno had a solution for this as well. There was a hand car wash in the underground that would do an inside-and-out car wash for just $120. He had the car done twice a month and enjoyed the feeling of climbing into his shining car every couple of weeks.

When Bruno lost his job at the bank and went to work at a credit union in the suburbs, lots of things changed. With a reduced salary, he had to recast their budget. The $240 monthly tab on car cleaning had to go.

Bruno signed up for a points card at his gas retailer and was soon earning points that he used to get free car washes. The exterior of his car looked good as new. The interior, however, looked...well...used.

Jodi suggested they pay their son, Thomas, $20 a week to clean the inside of the car. Thomas liked the idea but negotiated it up to $25 and set up a savings account for university.

Even paying Thomas for the interior work, Bruno was still saving $140 a month. Compounding at 7%, the new arrangement would save him $24,080 over the next 10 years. Bonus: Thomas was learning some great life lessons that would set him up for a lifetime of prosperity. Mostly around how to negotiate with his dad.

Car washes are an easy expense to eliminate entirely. A gas retailer loyalty program will provide enough points to keep you in free car washes for a lifetime. If you drive a large vehicle, you may have enough credits to cover car washes for your friends—or at least snag a couple of those aromatic pine-tree air fresheners.

Ingredients

- Go online to the various gasoline retailers and look at their points programs.

- See if they have a nifty keychain dongle that lets you tap the pump to pay, which saves fumbling for credit cards in a) searing heat, b) blowing snow or c) driving rain. The dongle routes the payment to your credit card, adds to your points to fund your car washes, saves the hassle of carrying and swiping a loyalty card and gets you back on the road faster.

- Pick the program you like based on program features and the chain that has locations that are handy for you.

- For interior cleaning, learn how to detail your car on YouTube. You may have some modest one-time costs for tools, like a crevice vacuum cleaner attachment (necessary for getting French fries out from that narrow, dark, too-skinny-for-your-hand place between your front seats and the centre console), but you'll save in the long run and have a better-smelling ride.

This recipe pairs nicely with a rewards credit card of your choosing. By connecting your payment dongle to your rewards credit card (you have one of those, right?), you can gather loyalty points on your card while saving for free car washes with your fuel points. It's like cheating.

Be careful to use your points to replace the car washes you were originally paying for. If you squander your points on ice cream bars, grape slushies and pepperoni sticks at the gas station convenience store, you will lose the financial benefits and still end up paying to wash your chariot.

> If you have a points surplus, use it for windshield washer fluid, windshield wiper blades or other useful car things you buy anyway.

Hearty Serving

- Two cars
- $12 per wash, two washes each per month = $48 monthly
- Joined loyalty program to get free washes
- Savings, $48 monthly

Light Serving

- One car
- $10 per wash, one wash per month
- Joined loyalty program to get free washes
- Savings, $10 monthly

Yield

Servings	Monthly Savings	10-Year Value × 173	20-Year Value × 521
Hearty	$48	$8,304	$25,008
Light	$10	$1,730	$5,210
Your info			

Wow! Took you 15 minutes to sign up for the program and you likely added at least a couple grand to your net worth 10 years out. Love it! But don't gloat over making this easy dish. Lock in your savings or debt reduction and move on to the next recipe! We have lots more chopping to do!

Traffic Ticket Tikka Masala $

It was a beautiful spring day. Lucy was driving back from a church fundraiser, singing an alto accompaniment to Old Blue Eyes.

The siren jolted her out of her private Sinatra concert, and she slowed and moved to the right to let the cop pass. But he didn't pass, he pulled in behind her, filling her rear-view mirror with flashing lights. Uh oh.

Her hands were shaking as she passed her licence and registration to the officer. He took everything back to his cruiser. Did he need to keep the lights flashing? So embarrassing. Apparently, Lucy had been driving 71 km/h in a 40 zone, earning her a $226 ticket.

Lucy was mad at herself for not being more careful; that money could have gone to the new sofa they were saving for. Stan suggested she fight the ticket. "Give it a shot; you never know," he advised.

Lucy went to court to fight the ticket and had it reduced to $103.75. As she was leaving the courthouse, Richard texted to say he had found a gently used couch on Kijiji for a lot less than Lucy and Brad were planning to spend. Lucy turned off the radio and hummed to herself all the way home, keeping her attention on the road. Sinatra was going to have to find another partner.

Is it just me, or are there always police and parking enforcement people around at the wrong time? A three-minute sprint to grab the dry cleaning: BAM! A trifle over the speed limit: POW!

The math on parking tickets is simple: paid parking is always a fraction of the cost of a fine, and if it means a bit of a walk, you get a free fitness bonus. If you do get a ticket, though, it's almost always worth fighting them. Same goes for speeding tickets. You'll almost always get a small reduction in the fine or demerit points just for showing up, looking earnest and owning up to your mistake.

Cashflow Cookbook

Ingredients

- Slow down, savour the drive, keep your temper on simmer and keep your money in your pocket.
- Leave the house 10 minutes earlier to reduce stress and the need to speed.
- Take a minute to pay for street parking each trip.
- Check the smartphone app store to see if there is a cool parking app for where you live that lets you find open spots, pay on your phone and monitor how much time is left on the meter. Some of them even let you extend your parking time right on your phone.
- For minor traffic tickets try fighting them on your own to save the ticket and possible increased insurance premiums—if you win and the ticket is thrown out, you'll have no insurance increase. If the conviction puts fewer points against your driver's licence, the change in insurance will be less. Worst case is that they leave the ticket as is.
- For larger tickets, look into one of the services that fights tickets for you.

> If you have been charged with impaired driving, dangerous driving or anything else major, put down this book and get professional legal help.

Hearty Serving
- Two cars
- One parking ticket per car (2 × $25) = $50 monthly
- Used paid street parking for every trip = $10 monthly, saving $40 monthly
- One $120 traffic ticket per year, equivalent to $10 monthly, raising insurance by $8 monthly
- Fought ticket to lower it to $60, saving $5 monthly and saving insurance increase of $8 monthly
- Savings, $53 monthly

Light Serving
- One car
- One $25 parking ticket monthly
- Used paid street parking for every trip = $5 monthly
- Savings, $20 monthly

Yield

Servings	Monthly Savings	10-Year Value × 173	20-Year Value × 521
Hearty	$53	$9,169	$27,613
Light	$20	$3,460	$10,420
Your info			

Some nice savings and a lot less stress from worrying about getting and paying for parking tickets. With traffic tickets, simply drive carefully to avoid them.

Car Insurance Clam Bake with Steamed Radiator

Jodi was pleased with the savings she had found by switching their home insurance to a new provider.

She may have been a little too excited by her success. When her car insurance renewal arrived a couple of weeks later she realized she should have included it as part of her earlier discussion with the home insurance company.

Her first instinct was to call her new home insurance company and add the car coverage. Instead, she did a little online comparison and got some competitive quotes for both car and home insurance. With those in hand she then called the new home insurer to get its quote on the insurance for their two vehicles. She went through each element of the insurance with the representative to ensure that she had the right coverage and that all applicable discounts were in place, given that both she and Bruno had safe driving records.

By combining the home and car insurance with the same company, Jodi saved over $70 a month and knew she had a competitive rate. She used the $70 to increase their monthly RESP contributions for their children.

Most of the time, your car insurance just sits there quietly, like the bag of spinach rotting at the back of your fridge.

That changes if you get into an accident, after which the details of your policy become strangely interesting, like a steaming bowl of shiitake risotto.

Book an hour to wade through the insurance company phone system, get to an agent and gently request their help to optimize your costs.

Ingredients

- Adequate liability insurance on your vehicle policy is always must, but older cars may be better suited to lower levels of comprehensive and collision insurance.

- Compare rates at different deductibles and pick the highest deductible you can afford, should you have a claim.
- Shop around for rates and coverage. Try one of the online car insurance quoting tools, such as Kanetix.ca or InsuranceHotline.com, or at least check with your current provider for the best rates and features. Work with an insurance broker if you prefer.
- Bundle home and car insurance for 10–15% savings. If you have a vacation property, add that in for bigger savings.
- Slow down, drive carefully and reduce premium-inflating traffic tickets.
- If you have university-aged kids away at school, call your insurance company and let them know—it will often lower the premium if the little darlings aren't actually using your car while they away.

> Always ensure you have proper coverage in place at all times.
> If your car's roadside assistance plan has expired, consider joining an automobile association to save on roadside towing and other emergency repairs. This gets you safe and vetted tows if you need them and offers discounts on car stuff, including insurance. It's worth the cost for the safety and peace of mind.

Hearty Serving

- Two cars (one newer), three drivers
- Total premium of $284 monthly
- Increased the deductibles from $500 to $1,000, saving $28 monthly
- Removed comprehensive coverage from older car, saving $19 monthly
- Shopped coverage like for like, saving $23 monthly
- New premium, $214 monthly
- Savings, $70 monthly

Light Serving

- One older car, one driver
- Total premium of $147 monthly
- Increased the deductible from $500 to $1,000, saving $14 monthly
- Bundled with home insurance, saving $19 monthly
- New premium, $114 monthly
- Savings, $33 monthly

Yield

Servings	Monthly Savings	10-Year Value × 173	20-Year Value × 521
Hearty	$70	$12,110	$36,470
Light	$33	$5,709	$17,193
Your info			

Not bad for a one-hour phone call every couple of years. Get the freed-up cashflow working for you with debt reduction or increased TFSA, RRSP or RESP contributions.

Devilled Driving Habits $ $ 🍸

Bruno and Jodi sometimes used each other's vehicles, depending on who was taking the dog to the groomer or doing the biweekly Costco run.

Jodi's minivan had a fuel consumption gauge. Over time, she noticed that when she drove, she averaged about 13 litres per 100 km, but Bruno averaged more like 16 L/100 km. That was a difference of more than 20%.

As she watched him drive, she noticed he accelerated rapidly and approached red lights at full steam, aggressively braking as he arrived at the intersection. He always seemed to be in a hurry, passing other cars on the highway and always exceeding the speed limit by a good margin.

Jodi checked their credit card records and saw that they spent over $4,000 per vehicle on gas each year. If she could get Bruno to drive more gently, they could save about $800 a year. Jodi wondered how to broach the topic.

A few weeks later, she spotted a newspaper article about the benefits of smooth driving and left it out for him. Luckily, he was interested, and the article sparked a conversation that ultimately got him to smooth out his driving and keep an eye on fuel consumption.

Their gas bills dropped, driving was less stressful, the brakes lasted longer and their dog didn't have to struggle to stay on the seat as Bruno drove.

Fast acceleration. Hard braking. Lurching forward and back. Ever follow someone like that? Any chance you drive like that?

A few simple changes to your driving style can easily save you 10% on gas and repairs, keep you out of court and offer your passengers (including the four-legged ones) a more comfortable ride.

Ingredients

- Accelerate gradually and smoothly.
- Look at traffic ahead and release the gas pedal if you see cars slowing. See if you can coast like that before braking. Usually, if you coast for a bit the problem ahead sorts itself out. Often there is no need to brake and then accelerate. Repeatedly.

- Likewise, brake lightly and smoothly.
- Combine trips to save total mileage.
- Don't carry extra junk in your car, especially heavy stuff. Your golf clubs don't need to be there full time.
- Keep your tires inflated to the correct pressure. Check your car manufacturer's recommendation, usually found on a label on the driver-side door jamb.
- Don't idle the car for more than a minute. Modern engines don't need to be warmed up.
- Slow down on the highway.

Do an internet search for eco-driving for more information. Cars use the least gas when driven at a constant, moderate speed. The less braking and accelerating, the better. Imagine an egg between your foot and the brake and another between your foot and the gas pedal. Easy does it. Of course, go ahead and scramble that egg if you need to avoid an accident.

You may be able to double the mileage between brake replacements, reduce tire wear and make lots of other parts last longer. Like anything else, 30 days makes a habit. If your car has a fuel consumption display, check it every now and again to see the difference driving style makes.

Extreme eco-driving enthusiasts (aka hyper-milers) do crazy things like taping over seams between body panels, removing side mirrors and wiper blades, even modifying the bodywork to make a car more "aero." For our purposes, let's just drive more carefully and leave our cars the way their makers intended them.

Hearty Serving

- Two cars
- Total expenses of $600 gas + $300 repairs = $900 monthly

- Learned better driving techniques, saving 10%
- Saving, $90 monthly

Light Serving

- One car
- Expenses of $200 gas + $50 repairs = $250 monthly
- Learned better driving techniques, saving 10%
- Savings, $25 monthly

Yield

Servings	Monthly Savings	10-Year Value × 173	20-Year Value × 521
Hearty	$90	$15,570	$46,890
Light	$25	$4,325	$13,025
Your info			

No investment required, just smoother, smarter and safer cruising. Get those savings driving some wealth—use them to reduce debt or increase monthly savings contributions *right now*.

Mall Trip Meringue

$ $ 🍸

Being a single working mother with two growing girls meant Vismaya was always short on time and money. Her ex-husband, Frank, was little help with the girls and was constantly late on support payments. His times caring for their daughters were fraught with drama and excitement...not always the positive kind.

Vismaya had become more efficient as a result. She constantly looked for ways to multitask and to stretch her budget. For example, she always did some comparison shopping online before heading to the stores.

One Saturday in December, after completing her online research, she and the girls headed to the mall. Traffic crawled, the girls bickered, the parking lot was jammed. After circling a few times, Vismaya signalled to turn in to an empty spot, only to have another driver zip in ahead of her, flipping her off as they did.

She held her temper, found another spot and headed into the packed mall for some linens and a few other household items. The girls had their own agenda and wouldn't leave until they each had a new shirt. To top it off, she found a big, fat $60 parking ticket on her windshield—the price of not spotting the handicapped space sign.

On the way home, it suddenly hit her: with just a couple of more clicks she could have purchased everything online. That was the day Vismaya became an online shopping convert. Better prices, no trips to the mall and, best of all, her weekends would be free for fun activities with her daughters.

Are shopping malls your idea of a good time? Nasty crowds, parking space battles, inflated prices and a food court designed to add nothing but fat, sugar and salt to your diet.

And that's before the cost of driving. The cheapest way to drive your car is, well, not at all. We have come to think that buying something involves driving ourselves to the item and then driving ourselves and the item back home. A bit odd really. And inefficient.

Cars & Transportation

Sometimes, we drive to the mall when we don't need anything and just look for things to buy. Then drive ourselves home, with or without more stuff. Even crazier.

Ingredients

- Consider whether you really need the item you're planning to get—don't shop just to shop.
- Can you walk or bike to a local store and skip the driving?
- Can you buy it online? Amazon is usually the price leader, but not always. Do a quick check between Amazon, leading retailers' online stores and warehouse clubs such as Costco, then look for used items on eBay, Kijiji or Craigslist.
- For clothing, try items on in the store to get the sizes right, and then next time save the trip and order from the same retailer online.
- Sign up for email updates from your favourite retailers. Savings can be significant—20, 30 even 40% isn't unusual. Be sure you set an email rule so the emails are routed to a shopping folder to keep the junk mail out of your inbox and to prevent impulse buying.

This recipe is so versatile, it could have gone in multiple chapters: It saves on product costs, gas, parking tickets, car repairs and your time. Plus, it might help tame the impulse buying that shopping malls are designed to encourage.

> Before you go online or to the store for something, do a quick check that you actually need the item. Maybe borrowing or renting will do the trick.

Hearty Serving

- Two cars, weekly mall trips
- Total expenses of $600 gas + $300 repairs = $900 monthly
- Reduced car use, saving 10%
- Savings, $90 monthly

Light Serving

- One car, occasional mall trips
- Expenses of $200 gas + $50 repairs = $250 monthly
- Reduced car use, saving 5%
- Savings, $12 monthly

Yield

Servings	Monthly Savings	10-Year Value × 173	20-Year Value × 521
Hearty	$90	$15,570	$46,890
Light	$12	$2,076	$6,252
Your info			

If you don't buy the item at all, you save the greenhouse gases on top of saving the expense of running your car. And by not sitting in traffic for an hour, you have time to get out for a run, clean up some work emails and still make it to the kids' soccer game.

Car Repair Ragout

Stan came home with a big load of groceries. On his final trip from car to kitchen, he closed the back hatch and glanced at the passenger side of his minivan. It was then that he saw it.

It looked like white horizontal streaks on the red van. Hmm. Perhaps a rogue shopping cart sideswiped his van while he was in the store? Whatever happened, it didn't look great and the cost to get it fixed would be taxing on his piano teacher's income. As he surveyed the damage, he realized the scratches weren't deep—in fact, it might be plastic or paint that actually got etched onto his vehicle.

Stan was about to call the dealership to get a quote on the body work when he looked over at the stove and remembered a very expensive lesson about a paperclip.

A quick search on YouTube revealed that paint scratches can often be dealt with using a scratch repair kit.

A $25 Canadian Tire scratch kit and an old rag worked like magic! Once the mark was gone, Stan rinsed off the residue, gave the van a good wax and it looked as good as, well, a faded red 2004 minivan. He had saved a couple of trips to the dealership and several hundred dollars. He even had most of his repair kit left for the next incident.

Whoops. You backed your ride into a post and now have a nasty dent in the plastic bumper. Your car dealer likely gave you a knowing smile and an estimate north of $1,500—enough to cancel some of your great savings work so far.

Or perhaps your dealer has said it's time for your cabin air filter to be replaced for $85. A trip to your local auto parts store will reveal that the filter itself is about $25. But who knows how to replace one? Only the dealer knows the sorcery necessary to repair dented bumpers and replace air filters...

Or is there another way?

Ingredients

- Use the magic of YouTube to reveal repair secrets like these and many more:
    - For dented minivan bumpers, try gently heating the bumper with a hair dryer, followed by some vigorous fist thumping from the inside and then the application of a bag of ice to freeze the bumper into position.
    - You can indeed replace your cabin air filter. It is likely hidden at the top of your glove box and can be replaced in about two minutes with no tools. Ask the internet.
- Don't be afraid to haggle on the price of repairs. Car repair is a competitive business and they want to keep you coming back.
- Follow your manufacturer's schedule for maintenance, and don't buy into "seasonal specials" unless they align with the maintenance schedule.
- Shop around for expensive replacement parts like tires. Checking two or three tire places, big-box stores and your dealer online will see price differences of 15% or more. Be sure to price the entire job, including new valves, installation and balancing. This research might take 30 minutes but it can save you $100–$200.

> If you are not comfortable doing a repair yourself, if the process looks too complex, if the fix might void your warranty or if it could compromise your safety, get it done at the dealer or other mechanic shop.
>
> If you're driving an Aston Martin, a Bentley or a Lambo, don't be bashing at dented fenders and slathering on scratch repair compound. Get the car to the dealer. Or, better still, trade it in on something more economical.

Hearty Serving

- Do it yourself on $100 of projects monthly
- Examples: replacing bulbs, batteries and cabin air filters or changing the oil
- Savings, $100 monthly

Light Serving

- Do it yourself on $50 of projects monthly
- Examples: removing scratches with polishing compound; replacing bulbs, cabin and engine air filters, and windshield wipers
- Savings, $50 monthly

Yield

Servings	Monthly Savings	10-Year Value × 173	20-Year Value × 521
Hearty	$100	$17,300	$52,100
Light	$50	$8,650	$26,050
Your info			

The joy of new knowledge, the satisfaction of doing it yourself and freed-up cashflow: all in a day's work. Get that free money working for you by preparing a delicious debt reduction.

Layered Commute Parfait

Richard had been working at his engineering job for about six months. The work was enjoyably challenging and he was proud to be part of creating a wave-power project that would help green the planet.

Less green, however, was Richard's commute. Driving his fossil burner more than 50 km each way added up to 25,000 km a year. Apart from environmental concerns, Richard realized the gas, parking and repair bills were blooming like mouldy bread in a warm cupboard. Richard posted a notice on his employer's online message board to see if any of his co-workers might want to share the commute.

Richard got a response from Robin, who lived in the same neighbourhood and worked only six cubicles away. Robin worked a four-day week and was happy to share gas and parking costs Monday to Thursday. Richard negotiated a deal to work from home on Fridays, allowing a better lifestyle and saving a further 20% on commuting costs. With two people in the car, they could use the carpool lanes, which saved about 10 minutes each way on the trip. More green in his wallet. More green for the planet.

Doing the math, Richard realized savings of 60% of gas and parking costs, a total of nearly $300 monthly. Richard told Stan the great news and they immediately increased their mortgage payments by $300 per month.

The average Canadian commute is 25 minutes each way, and 80% of people drive to work. For many, the daily commute is the biggest single use of their car. Often the car has only one occupant.

With a bit of organizing and planning, there are numerous ways to pare away commuting costs. Although we are programmed to drive ourselves to work and back five days a week, take a moment to consider some alternatives. As we will see, the savings are worth it.

Ingredients
- Can you work closer to where you live? Or vice versa? Does your employer have another location closer to your home? Can

you work there some of the time? If you can get close enough, maybe you don't even need a car.

- Set up a carpool—post a notice at work and online or try the new Waze app carpool feature to find neighbours who drive in the same direction.

- Work from home one day a week—save 20% of your commuting costs and use the former drive time for productive work. If you have a particularly agreeable employer, maybe you can work from home most of the time, sell your car and just take an Uber or Zipcar in to work occasionally.

- With Uber, look at using the Pool and Express Pool option, sharing your ride and sometimes adding a short walk to save 50% or more on UberX rates.

- Look at using transit if you can—compare costs with driving. It might be worth doing even a day or two a week.

- Ride your bike three seasons of the year if possible—see if your workplace or one nearby has bike storage and showers. Bonus: your commute and your gym trip become one.

Not all of these ideas will work for you. But can one of them work, even for one or two days a week? Challenge yourself to find a creative commuting recipe you like.

Hearty Serving

- One person commuting
- Spending $200 gas + $300 parking + $50 maintenance + $100 tolls
- Total commuting costs, $650 monthly
- Carpooled to save 50%
- New cost, $325 monthly
- Savings, $325 monthly

Light Serving

- One person commuting
- Spending $150 gas + $50 maintenance
- Total commuting costs, $200 monthly
- Worked from home to save 20%
- New cost, $160 monthly
- Savings, $40 monthly

Yield

Servings	Monthly Savings	10-Year Value × 173	20-Year Value × 521
Hearty	$325	$56,225	$169,325
Light	$40	$6,920	$20,840
Your info			

Incredible savings, well worth taking the time to find a lower-cost option. If you have two or more commuters in the family, look for a solution for each one separately. You may even be able to boil things down enough to shift from two cars to one.

SUV Succotash $ $ $ 🍴 🍴

Bruno and Jodi's neighbour pulled up in a small, sporty new car, keen to show it off. Bruno admired the car and liked the idea of something smaller, easier on gas and simpler to park in the city. However, he needed his SUV for family trips and getting everyone around.

Bruno and Jodi talked it over during dinner. Jodi pointed out they only had two kids and her minivan, or pretty much any vehicle, can get four people around. Bruno had never looked at it this way before. Rather than thinking of the cars as his SUV and Jodi's minivan, all they really needed was one small car for commuting and a larger one to get them all around on the weekends.

Bruno strolled out to the driveway and had a long look at his SUV. It really was overkill. He then stared at the minivan. Nowhere near as cool as his SUV. But who cares? Jodi loved him no matter what he drove. There would be some ribbing from his friends, but he was no stranger to sharp repartee. He grinned as he thought up a few snappy comebacks.

Getting a new vehicle was a great opportunity for savings and likely a chance to help the environment. It was also an opportunity to be better role models to their sons, Thomas and Ken.

Bruno did some research and then went to the dealership and traded in his luxury landship for a small two-year-old commuter car. He got $22,000 cash back on the deal, which he applied to their mortgage. He would also save nearly $150 a month on gas, $74 a month on insurance and about $85 or so in repairs. He wondered why he had ever bought such a barge in the first place.

He applied the monthly savings to increased RESP contributions and realized, with satisfaction, they would fully max out the government grant contribution to the plan. It felt great to have the boys' education covered and he loved the idea of the government sharing the load.

Have you been biting off more car than you can economically chew?

OK, so you have kids. With lots of stuff. And friends. And a couple of dogs. And maybe it snows where you live and a big vehicle with all-wheel drive is helpful.

But how often do both parents have all the kids, the stuff, the friends and the dogs in the car when it is snowing?

Rather than thinking of the cars as belonging one to each parent, think of them as a fleet—a large and a small car, used by whoever has the need for the extra room that day.

Ingredients

- Keep one larger vehicle for moving the kids and the stuff, and a small commuter car for the spouse who is not on shepherd duty.
- Have the little darlings walk, bike or take public transit to school or their programs if that is safe and workable where you live.
- Can one spouse bike or take transit to work and get rid of a car entirely?
- Could the "big" car be a minivan or a wagon instead of a gas-hungry SUV?
- Buy gently used two- or three-year-old cars instead of new ones—let someone else pay the depreciation while you get another six years+ of trouble-free driving.
- Keep your cars longer. Decent, well-maintained cars can easily last 250,000 km.
- If you find yourself resisting change in this area, review the yield table below and then revisit this ingredient list.

Hearty Serving

- Two SUVs
- Replaced one SUV with economy car
- Savings of $200 in gas, $50 in insurance, $50 in repairs and $200 is payments
- Savings, $500 monthly

Light Serving

- Two mid-sized cars
- Replaced one mid-sized car with economy car
- Savings of $100 in gas, $25 in insurance, $25 in repairs and $100 in payments
- Savings, $250 monthly

Yield

Servings	Monthly Savings	10-Year Value × 173	20-Year Value × 521
Hearty	$500	$86,500	$260,500
Light	$250	$43,250	$130,250
Your info			

Big difference! Use *Consumer Reports* or the *Lemon-Aid Car Guide* to help find cars with great reliability and lower cost of ownership.

Parking Lot Perogies

$ $ $ 🍴

Vismaya pulled into the underground parking lot at her office.

Unfortunately, at her job level, free parking wasn't provided, so every day she took the ticket from the machine on the way in and paid on the way out. Every so often, she would gather up all the stubs from her car and throw them in the recycling bin.

As she gathered them one day, she thought about her parking costs. At $21 for each of 21 working days a month, she was spending an astounding $441 for parking every month. This was a huge expenditure she had largely overlooked.

Vismaya asked her colleagues for ideas. To her surprise, she found that most of them didn't park under the building. "Way too expensive," said Grant, who worked in her department. "I park at an apartment building a block away. I set up a deal for $220 a month in cash."

The next day, Grant walked Vismaya over to the apartment building and introduced her to the superintendent. He signed her up for the same deal.

Vismaya insisted on taking Grant to lunch to thank him. She raised a brow when he ordered an appetizer, soup and an entrée. As he started his tiramisu and sipped his cappuccino, she couldn't resist a word.

"Sure you got enough to eat, Grant?"

"I'm saving you $221 a month and you want to buy me half a lunch?!" They grinned at each other as they left the restaurant.

Vismaya spent part of her first month's savings on Grant's comprehensive lunch. The second month's savings went to new winter boots for the girls, and then she applied the ongoing savings to their RESP.

If you pay to park for work each day, take some time to consider cheaper alternatives.

Paying, say, $15 a day for parking doesn't seem like a big deal. But at $15 for each of 21 working days a month, that is a monthly bill of $315, or $3,780 a year. At $30 per day it adds up to $630 a month.

Ouch. Kind of like forgetting to use oven mitts.

Ingredients

- Do an internet search for "find monthly parking" in your city.
- Use a parking app like Best Parking—it displays available monthly parking spots with prices on a map around your workplace. Awesome!
- Can you park for less near transit and use that for the last part of the commute?
- Does your building offer a discount for paying for parking monthly rather than daily?
- Visit nearby condos and apartment buildings to see if they have extra spaces to rent.
- At the very least, do a stroll one lunch hour and check the rates on other lots near your workplace.

Hearty Serving

- Two cars commuting
- One car paying $30 daily for parking × 21 days = $630 monthly
- One car paying $20 daily for parking × 21 days = $420 monthly
- Total parking costs, $1,050 monthly
- Found two new parking spots at local condos for a total of $520 monthly
- Savings, $530 monthly

Light Serving

- One car commuting
- One car paying $20 daily for parking × 21 days = $420 monthly
- Found a new parking spot at local condo for $220 monthly
- Savings, $200 monthly

Yield

Servings	Monthly Savings	10-Year Value × 173	20-Year Value × 521
Hearty	$530	$91,690	$276,130
Light	$200	$34,600	$104,200
Your info			

Wow. Making this change might take an hour of research and a five- or 10-minute walk to your new parking spot each day. You may need to season the math slightly if you drive to work only some days of the month. Be sure to do the research for each car commuting.

Serve with an increased monthly car or mortgage payment, or savour the rising balance in your savings account.

The Take-Away Container

Cars are cool and convenient but they take a huge bite out of your income. Try adding up the total cost of running your car for a year.

This section's 10 recipes can save a potential total of $112,796 for our Light Servings and $320,223 for the Hearty Servings over 10 years when invested at 7%:

✓ **Get the app.** Use navigation apps to cut commuting time by routing around traffic jams.

✓ **Stop paying for car washes.** Sign up for a gas retailer loyalty program to get free washes.

✓ **Tackle your tickets.** Drive responsibly and pay up front for parking. Fighting traffic tickets is worth the time. Avoiding them is better.

✓ **Shop your insurance.** Look for the right insurance for your situation, combine with your home insurance, see if annual billing is cheaper, notify them when kids move out.

✓ **Drive gently.** Learn eco-driving techniques to crush fuel and repair costs.

✓ **Stay home and click.** Do your shopping from home to purée fuel and parking costs, hassle and time.

✓ **Reduce the repairs.** Shop around for the best repair cost and learn some basic maintenance you can do yourself.

✓ **Creative commuting.** Bike, walk, carpool, take transit and/or work from home.

✓ **Downsize.** What vehicles do you really need?

✓ **Park for less.** Look at alternative parking options.

Continuously look at your recurring transportation costs to find ways to improve. Check out the Ingredients section at Cashflow-Cookbook.com for tested products and services that can help.

Food & Drink

FOOD COSTS CONSUME ABOUT 13% of the average Canadian budget, so it's worthwhile to convert some of those calories back into wealth.

Since your health is much more important that your wealth, let's focus on financial recipes that are beneficial to both.

Changes in these areas can make a difference:

— Groceries: shop healthy and save
— Choices: save with generic and frozen food
— Daily habits: ditch soft drinks and coffee
— Meal prep: make it faster, healthier and cheaper
— Bottled water: rethink hydration convenience
— Snacks: prepare and save
— Lists: buy what you need

But let's not take the fun out as we reduce the costs. Some simple changes can make a big difference with minimal sacrifice.

Battered Bottled Water $ 🍸

Thomas was struggling for a topic for his environmental studies class. Jodi was getting set to fly to Calgary to spend some time with her sister. Thomas followed his mom around the house asking her for ideas.

"Why not do something on all the discarded plastic from water bottles?" Jodi suggested. "I was just watching a show last night about how much waste they create."

After Bruno and Thomas said goodbye to Jodi at airport security, they walked through the airport, passing a busy newsstand where people were lined up to buy newspapers, drinks and chewing gum. Bruno and Thomas zeroed in on the bottled water in the hands of many customers.

"Why not do a report on how much bottled water gets purchased in one hour from just this one location?" suggested Bruno.

So for the next hour, Thomas sat across from the newsstand and counted the bottles purchased there. As they left the airport, Thomas stopped at the water fountain just down from the newsstand for some fresh, cool, free water. Thomas and his dad grinned at each other.

At home, Thomas did the calculations and figured out how much people spend, how much money the bottling companies make and how much plastic has to be recycled.

Get out your fancy stand mixer and whip up some ethylene glycol with a dash of terephthalic acid and you can make a big pot of polyethylene terephthalate. Mmm! Just kidding—don't try this in your kitchen. Or even your garage.

What that stuff is, is a type of clear plastic usually known as PET. We can blow-mould this plastic into bottles, fill them with water (often tap water) and truck them to distribution centres. Some of them go to catering companies that sell them at baseball games for $6 a throw. Many of them get trucked to grocery stores. People buy them by the case and drive them home in their minivans. The bottles are a bit hard to store, so they usually get stacked up in the kitchen, often within 10 feet of the kitchen faucet. Maybe reread this paragraph. Now shake your head.

If you regularly buy bottled water, you may also notice that people at your house don't always finish their bottles of water, which means you dump the leftovers down the sink, where it ultimately heads out to the ocean to be with the rest of the water. And of course, plenty of those plastic water bottles don't make it to the recycling plant so they eventually head to the ocean too to join the tonnes already swirling around out there.

Bottled water is not useless, but let's save it for situations where it's actually needed, such as in the aftermath of disasters, when it saves lives by allowing people to avoid contaminated local water, and in other circumstances where safe water is unavailable.

Ingredients

- Stop buying cases of bottled water for home use.
- Skip the carbonated bottled water too.
- Carry a reusable bottle and fill it from your tap and public fountains instead. Canada has some of the best tap water in the world.
- Consider using the many free sources of clean water—fountains and faucets in locations like your workplace, schools, gym, malls and other public areas.

Hearty Serving

- Family of five
- Buying four cases of bottled water for a total of $20 monthly
- Buying six one litre bottles of sparking water for a total of $24 monthly
- Buying 20 single bottles at $1.50 each for a total of $30 monthly
- Total water spending, $74 monthly
- Switched to tap water for $0 monthly
- Savings, $74 monthly

Light Serving

- Single person
- Buying one bottled water with lunch at $2, 21 working days each month, $42 monthly
- Total water spending, $42 monthly
- Switched to tap water for $0 monthly
- Savings, $42 monthly

Yield

Servings	Monthly Savings	10-Year Value × 173	20-Year Value × 521
Hearty	$74	$12,802	$38,554
Light	$42	$7,266	$21,882
Your info			

OK, not a ticket to instant wealth, but you can still enjoy a good cashflow boost while saving wear and tear on the minivan, reducing garbage and recycling, teaching your kids about green living and helping our marine friends to a healthier life. That's a buffet of goodness.

Big-Brand Bourguignon on a Bed of Je Ne Sais Quoi

Lucy was excited to go to her book club meeting. This month's read was a murder mystery, and unlike many of the previous selections, she had actually finished it. She felt unusually well prepared and was looking forward to a robust discussion.

The dinner format was a potluck and her friend Sandy brought an incredible pasta salad that had the group raving. In fact, they were more interested in the mystery of the salad than the murder in the book.

"I call it my generic pasta salad," Sandy laughed.

"Generic? It's delicious!" countered Lucy.

Sandy explained that all the ingredients were generic or house-brand products from the supermarket: It tastes 20% better than most pasta salads, but the ingredients are 20% cheaper.

Lucy had never paid much attention to the generic brands, but on her next trip to the grocery store, her cart was filled with the tell-tale plain labels.

Years of brand advertising has built our Pavlovian reflexes such that we think of brand names almost before we think of the actual product we need to buy. Is it even possible that a product can clean, taste, foam or garnish properly without the labels we are so familiar with?

The cost of generic products averages about 25% less that nationally advertised brands. So why not splurge $1.69 on one tube of toothpaste or $2.69 on one jar of spaghetti sauce and find out? Worst case, you are out a couple of bucks. Best case, you have a new favourite and 25% savings on that part of your grocery bill. Forever.

Ingredients

- Try the generic products in each category, from canned and frozen foods to household needs like toilet paper, paper towels and garbage bags.

- Get a *Consumer Reports* online subscription and check their reviews of generics to save your own testing.
- Check pricing when you shop; sometimes the national brands are on sale, making them cheaper than the generics. There's no reason to go generic if old faithful is on sale.
- Make a list on your smartphone so you know which generic products made the grade. And share the list with any family members who help with the shopping.

Invest some time to research generic products. After all, you can't judge a can of beans by its label.

Hearty Serving

- Family of six
- Grocery bill of $1,500 monthly
- Switched $300 worth to generics, saving 25%
- New bill of $1,425 monthly
- Savings, $75 monthly

Light Serving

- Single person
- Grocery bill of $250 monthly
- Switched $80 worth to generics, saving 25%
- New bill of $230 monthly
- Savings, $20 monthly

Yield

Servings	Monthly Savings	10-Year Value × 173	20-Year Value × 521
Hearty	$75	$12,975	$39,075
Light	$20	$3,460	$10,420
Your info			

Not bad for some easy brand substitutions. Keep experimenting to find generics you like. Lock in the benefit by increasing debt or savings payments by the amount you save.

Frozen Food Frittata $ $ 🍸

Vismaya was picking up a few things at the grocery store. She needed some fruit, vegetables and a few other items. She was reaching for some ready-made smoothies when she heard a voice from behind her.

"Don't buy the bottled smoothies. Too expensive and loaded with preservatives."

"Um, and...you would be...?" asked Vismaya of the handsome stranger.

"Sorry, I'm William. Much cheaper and healthier to buy frozen fruit and just blend it yourself with some almond milk. I add some protein powder post workout." Vismaya thought he might have flexed ever so slightly when he said that.

"I'm Vismaya; nice to meet you. Do you offer grocery tips to every stranger in the store?" she asked coyly.

"Not every stranger," said William, his eyes locking hers. "If you have coffee with me next week, I'll give you more tips on frozen fruit."

"Tell me now," offered Vismaya, "and I'll think about it."

"OK." William looked into her cart. "Lose those ready-made oatmeal packets and buy the bulk rolled oats. Nuke some frozen fruit and add it to the oatmeal. Awesome, and much cheaper. How is Saturday morning at 10, at the coffee shop just around the corner?"

Vismaya smiled and nodded.

William normally shunned coffee places and instead brewed his own at home, but he had a feeling this particular coffee break might be worth the investment.

Ever spend a wonderful day cleaning out your fridge? Didn't think so.

Rooting through packages of decomposing matter, questioning the expiry dates, the contents or perhaps even why you bought it in the first place sure makes you appreciate why you procrastinated on the clean-up!

Spending a pile on groceries, then discarding them as toxic sludge just a few short months or even weeks later is no one's idea of a good time. So what if you could buy the groceries cheaper in the first place, reduce the waste and prolong the life of the leftovers?

Well, this magic exists, and it is known as "frozen food." Making some in-store comparisons, you will see that frozen food can range from 10% cheaper (strawberries) to 30% cheaper (chicken) to 50% cheaper (juice). And that is just savings on the purchase price. Reducing wasted food provides gourmet-level savings.

Plus, in cold climates like Canada, fresh produce in the winter is expensive and often tastes like the Styrofoam it's packaged on.

Let's assume that meat, fruit, vegetables and juice are approximately 40% of your grocery bill and that switching to frozen can save 30%. To be conservative, let's assume we will switch only half to frozen and that the savings are therefore only 15%.

Ingredients
- Experiment with buying more frozen fruit, vegetables and meat.
- Defrost only what you need; keep the rest carefully wrapped and frozen to reduce waste.

Hearty Serving
- Family of six
- Grocery bill of $1,500 monthly
- Meat, fruit, vegetables and juice are 40% of the bill, or $600
- Switched half of this to frozen to save 15%
- New grocery cost, $1,410 monthly
- Savings, $90 monthly

Light Serving
- Single professional
- Grocery bill of $250 monthly
- Meat, fruit and vegetables are 40% of the bill, or $100
- Switched half of this to frozen to save 15%
- New grocery cost, $235 monthly
- Savings, $15 monthly

Yield

Servings	Monthly Savings	10-Year Value × 173	20-Year Value × 521
Hearty	$90	$15,570	$46,890
Light	$15	$2,595	$7,815
Your info			

Not massive savings, but fewer smelly, mysterious packages in the fridge, less food waste and a smaller bag of compost to discard each week.

Prepared Food Purée $ $ 🍴 🍴

Frank was struggling. Between declining revenues for his construction business and his support payments for his children, his chequing account was overdrawn.

For the first few months after the divorce, Frank ate dinner out or grabbed takeout on the way home. It was fast and easy, but expensive.

Frank was forced to learn to shop and that involved making trips to that new frontier—the grocery store. Even after weeks of practice, he still cut an awkward path through the aisles. A time lapse video would show him executing several circumnavigations of the store to complete the ritual.

He discovered a new section with fully prepared foods: meatballs, lasagna, shepherd's pie and more, a huge variety of dinners that just needed heating. What could be easier? It had to be cheaper than dining out.

Frank filled his cart with the microwaveable packages and headed for the checkout. The cashier scanned them and told Frank the total. He fumed—it couldn't possibly have added up that quickly. Frank paid and stormed out of the store, cursing under his breath. The cashier shook her head, wondering why people bought expensive prepared foods full of preservatives and sodium and missed the fun of learning to cook their own meals.

Simple advice: Stay on the outside aisles of the grocery store rather than the middle aisles. The perimeter includes fruits and vegetables, breads, meat, fish, eggs and dairy products. The middle aisles include prepared foods, fat- and sugar-rich snacks, soda, cookies, crackers, sour keys, chocolate peanut butter cups, and, well, you get the idea.

In prepared foods, I am including ones that have been chopped, sliced, peeled and assembled for you, like fruit platters, sliced mushrooms and kale salads. Compare prices per pound and you will find that you are paying a premium of 20–50% for someone else to do some washing, chopping and packaging. If you are able, why not do some of your own prep work and save?

Prepared foods also include the ones where someone else made the sauces, did the frying and added the MSG, salt and sugar. Like the frozen meatballs, pre-made lasagna and boxed chicken wings. This stuff clogs both your arteries and your cashflow. Head to the perimeter of the store and save your money, your waistline and, maybe, your life.

Prepared foods make up over 22% of the average American grocery budget, so it's worth doing your own seasoning, grilling and mixing, even if you have to learn those skills first.

Ingredients

- Reduce consumption of prepared foods for health and financial benefits.
- Google simple recipes and learn to make a few basic dishes.
- Try entering the ingredients in your fridge, plus the word "recipe" and hit search—you will find recipes to make a meal with what you have or build the list of what you need to go buy.
- Peel, chop, season and assemble foods yourself.
- Try making a large batch of a dish and then freezing ready-to-go portions so you have a selection ready to heat and serve.

Hearty Serving

- Family of six
- Grocery bill of $1,500 monthly
- Switched $300 worth to non-prepared foods, saving about 30%
- New bill, $1,400 monthly
- Savings, $100 monthly

Light Serving

- Single person
- Grocery bill of $200 monthly
- Switched $60 worth to non-prepared foods, saving about 30%
- New bill, $180 monthly
- Savings, $20 monthly

Yield

Servings	Monthly Savings	10-Year Value × 173	20-Year Value × 521
Hearty	$100	$17,300	$52,100
Light	$20	$3,460	$10,420
Your info			

Great savings of cash, MSG, salt, sugar, fat, butylated hydroxytoluene and several other unpronounceable chemicals.

Meat Reduction Marinara $ $ 🍸

William was at the grocery store picking up a few things. He was a careful shopper and an athlete and thought of his groceries more by their category (protein, fat and carbohydrates) than by the actual appeal of the food. He tossed a 12-pack of chicken breasts into his cart and headed for the rice section.

"Not a good idea," said a voice from behind.

William spun around, recognizing Vismaya, the beautiful shopper he had met at the store a few weeks earlier. They had been on a couple of coffee dates since, and things were starting to progress.

"I thought I was the only one who offered grocery advice to strangers," William smiled.

"Clearly we're not strangers," said Vismaya, her dark eyes meeting his in a protracted gaze.

"You need to get the meat out of your diet," she said. "Tough on the environment and your arteries. Don't even get me started on animal cruelty. And aren't you the one trying to optimize your grocery costs?"

"Hmm," said William, "where will I get my protein?"

"Lots of places. Beans are great; I use them in all kinds of dishes. I use tofu as well. If you cook it right, you would swear it was meat, but far healthier."

"But does it taste as good?" asked William.

"No one cooks better vegan meals than me. Wait, are you angling for a dinner invitation?"

"Is Thursday night at seven OK?" offered William, taken with his own swagger.

Vismaya shook her head and laughed.

"Bring wine. 173 Balsam Avenue. Don't be late." She turned and headed down aisle 12. She was looking forward to the dinner and wondered how he would relate to her kids.

William dropped the chicken breasts back into the freezer and headed for the tofu.

According to Planet Money, meat makes up 22% of a typical grocery bill. And the evidence continues to pile up that moving to a more plant-based diet is a healthy choice. Going all the way to vegetarian or vegan meals is a personal choice, but reducing meat by, say, 30%

is good for both wallet and arteries. Time to put a steak in the ground. Sorry.

Whether it's to help animals, save the planet, improve your health or save money, reducing the carnivorous component of your groceries is worth a try. Think of fruits and vegetables as the mainstay and meat more as an accompaniment.

Ingredients

- Move to smaller meat portions at each meal—3 oz. is enough.
- Have a couple of vegetarian or vegan days each week.
- Start exploring healthier recipes.
- Try some vegetarian or vegan restaurants to tame your dining out bills and get inspiration for your own cooking.

Like anything else, 30 days makes a habit. With food, we tend to crave the foods we eat most. Focus on meat dishes and your shopping cart will steer itself in that direction. Eat more fruits and vegetables and your food fantasies will switch to big salads.

Hearty Serving

- Family of six
- Grocery bill of $1,500 monthly, $300 of it meat
- Switched $150 of meat to $50 of veggies and grains
- New bill, $1,400 monthly
- Savings, $100 monthly

Light Serving

- Single person
- Grocery bill of $400 monthly, $100 of it meat
- Switched $50 of meat to $20 of veggies and grains
- New bill, $370 monthly
- Savings, $30 monthly

Yield

Servings	Monthly Savings	10-Year Value × 173	20-Year Value × 521
Hearty	$100	$17,300	$52,100
Light	$30	$5,190	$15,630
Your info			

Improve your net worth, spruce up your cardiovascular system, reduce global warming and prevent a few furry or feathered friends from suffering. Almost too good to be true.

Sale Bin Salsa

$ $ ⚱ ⚱ ⚱

Stan was about to leave for the grocery store when he got a call from Brad, his father, looking for something to do. Stan suggested his dad join him for the shopping trip and he jumped at the chance. Stan liked being with his dad but he would ensure that he had a more comprehensive activity plan for his own retirement.

Stan checked his list while Brad manned the cart. As they headed to the household section, Stan grabbed an eight-pack of name brand toilet paper and placed it in the cart.

"Not in my cart!" said Brad sternly.

"Dad! It's not your cart."

"The hell it isn't!"

Stan shook his head. At 32 he was getting TP lectures from his dad.

"You missed the house brand on sale on the shelf just below. Grocery stores always put the pricey brands at eye level. Look just above and below for the deals!" said Brad, clearly, well, on a roll.

"Dad, that is a 48-pack, I don't need that much TP. I will look like an idiot walking out with that!"

"What do you mean you don't need that much? It's toilet paper! It's not like cigarettes. People don't quit using it. It doesn't go bad. You'd be paying 50% less! Next week the toothpaste will be on sale. That's how you save!"

His dad had a point. The 48-pack went in the cart in place of the small package. On the way out of the store, his dad carried three grocery bags while Stan wrestled with the toilet paper monolith. They were almost at the car when they heard someone shouting at them.

"Whoa Stan! Dude, have you been hitting that burrito place again? Are you even going to make it to band practice tonight?!"

It was Trevor, the drummer in Stan's band. Why couldn't it have been toothpaste on sale this week?

On most shopping trips you can score a few items on sale, like cans of black beans for 30% off, or maybe your favourite toothpaste has shed a buck from its usual price. Not bad, but no one ever got rich on occasional savings on beans and toothpaste.

What you really need are those kinds of discounts on most of your groceries, forever. Why not actually make that happen?

Grocery stores run on very thin margins, meaning they can't afford to offer large discounts all the time on all the stuff you need. So they sprinkle them around to entice you in the door on the sale items, and then make their money on the rest.

But what happens when we turn that around? Let's focus our buying on the sale items, switching brands or even products to get to those 30–50% discounts. If the sale items are ones that keep, why not stock up with a few weeks' supply? Paper towels, frozen vegetables, garbage bags, canned goods and coffee are all good candidates to buy when the price drops. Generally, these kinds of bulk non-perishables are also great to load up on at warehouse clubs.

Experiment with your perishable consumption trends to ensure that you and your family can take down the large format containers. A six-litre jug of ketchup, for example, is a deal only if you use it before it turns into a vat of nasty brown gunk.

Ingredients

- Stock up when non-perishable items go on sale.
- Substitute similar products that are on sale. If you are seeking frozen blueberries and frozen raspberries are on sale, be bold and switch!
- Keep a smartphone list of well-stocked items or a pantry picture so as not to over-buy anything.

> Pick up the grocery store's weekly flyer on your way into the store and adjust your list and meal plans around sale items.

Hearty Serving

- Family of six
- Grocery bill of $1,500 monthly
- Switched to buying $300 worth at 33% off
- New bill, $1,400 monthly
- Savings, $100 monthly

Light Serving

- Single person
- Grocery bill of $250 monthly
- Switched to buying $60 worth at 33% off
- New bill, $230 monthly
- Savings, $20 monthly

Yield

Servings	Monthly Savings	10-Year Value × 173	20-Year Value × 521
Hearty	$100	$17,300	$52,100
Light	$20	$3,460	$10,420
Your info			

These are slow-cooker savings, but as you can see, they still add up over time.

Grocery List Ganache $ $ 🍸 🍸

Jodi was off visiting her mother and had loaded up Bruno with a day of errands: drop the dog off at the groomer, take a couple of pairs of shoes for repair, pick up the dry cleaning and get some groceries.

He got the first three items done and was headed for the grocery store when the groomer called. The good news was that the dog was ready; the bad news was that they were closing in an hour.

Bruno raced through the grocery aisles, grabbing lettuce and celery, canned soup and pasta. He tossed in a cool dish scrubber that holds the soap right in the handle. Waiting in line, he added a couple of home renovation magazines, a pack of gum and a nifty keychain flashlight.

He made it to the groomer just in time to pick up his dog. They apologized for going a bit deep with the clippers; the dog was essentially hairless. Rookie groomer, apparently. At least, thought Bruno, Sparky wouldn't need clipping for a while.

Back at home, Thomas and Ken helped him unpack.

"Another dish scrubber?" asked Ken. "We just got a new one. Wait—what the hell did you do to the dog?"

"Dad, you said we're making quiche—where are the eggs?" asked Thomas.

Bruno was crestfallen. He opened the produce drawer in the fridge to load in the celery and lettuce but there was no room. The existing celery and lettuce were taking up all the space.

"What will we have for dinner?" asked Thomas.

"How about spaghetti?" offered Bruno. "Everyone likes spaghetti."

"We have no sauce," lamented Ken. Thomas called for pizza.

The following week, Jodi cleaned out the fridge, shaking her head at the rubber celery and wilted lettuce. "All he had to do was make a list," she mumbled.

Stop me if you've heard this one: your cart is almost full, you're cutting it close to get out of the store in time to drive someone to a piano lesson and BAM! Are those cookies actually half price? Should I just grab that block of cheese in case the kids get hungry after school? Hello, check out that candy display!

We all know how this ends. The cookies are gone 10 minutes after the kids find them, and that block of cheese takes the place of the mouldy one you bought a couple of weeks ago.

The easy lesson is to shop with a list. Less waste, fewer unneeded items and food that fits a healthy meal plan. Group the list by food areas in the store to save zipping from one end of the store to the other. It's one thing to buy milk, yogurt, cheese, strawberries, blueberries and bananas. It takes twice as long to shop for milk, strawberries, yogurt, blueberries, cheese and then bananas.

Using a shopping list is an easy way to knock 10% off your grocery bill. You'll use the ingredients you already have, avoid buying stuff you don't need and help prevent impulse buying. For the math below, we will go with a conservative 7% savings.

Ingredients

- Take a moment to create a shopping list, or try some of the shopping list apps from the App Store or Google Play, including ones from the grocery stores themselves.
- Spend some time planning your meals for the week, so you know what ingredients you will need.
- Before you head to the store, take a good look at what's in the fridge and the cupboards.
- Buy only what you need for that week's meals.
- Don't shop on an empty stomach.
- Keep the grocery list stuck to the fridge and train your family to add items they use up.

> Planning a week's meals also helps you implement the Meat Reduction Marinara recipe.

Hearty Serving

- Family of six
- Grocery bill of $1,500 month
- Used a list and didn't shop when hungry to save 7%
- New grocery cost, $1,395 monthly
- Savings, $105 monthly

Light Serving

- Single professional
- Grocery bill of $250 monthly
- Used a list and didn't shop when hungry to save 7%
- New grocery cost, $232 monthly
- Savings, $17 monthly

Yield

Servings	Monthly Savings	10-Year Value × 173	20-Year Value × 521
Hearty	$105	$18,165	$54,705
Light	$17	$2,941	$8,857
Your info			

Buy only what you need for less food waste, less grocery store drama and better health—and maybe even retire a few months earlier.

Sweet & Sour Snacks in a Belly Fat Confit $ $ 🍸

Bruno's buddy Glen invited him over to watch the football game. Glen was always coming up with new schemes, and Bruno enjoyed hearing about his latest business venture and his innovative way of seeing things.

They each cracked an opening beer, laid $20 on the coffee table for their bet and settled in to watch the game, talking work, investments and families during the commercials.

As they swigged their second beers, Glen started making popcorn. He grabbed a microwaveable bowl and lid and poured in some popping corn.

"Hey, Glen, not sure you heard, but they have this new-fangled thing called microwave popcorn," Bruno teased.

"Or, you could buy it in bulk, throw it in a microwavable bowl and stop wasting money," Glen shot back.

While the popcorn popped, Glen explained that bulk popcorn is about one-seventh the cost of the packaged microwave stuff and has less salt, less fat and more fibre.

"And it tastes the same, maybe even better," said Glen, grabbing a handful and kicking back for the second half.

"Hope your savings cover your bet, because those Eskimos are going down!"

The Snack Monster takes many forms. If feeding money into snack vending machines at work is part of your daily ritual, you have an opportunity to improve both your health and your finances.

The cost of machine snacks is at least double the cost of buying the same snacks in bulk at a warehouse club or bulk food store, and online ordering is likely cheaper still. But before you open your laptop, let's think about taking this all one step further.

Consider the fact that the craving for that next snack likely came from the addictive effects of your last fat- and sugar-laden snack.

Think about breaking the habit entirely with a move to healthier snacks.

Ingredients

- Instead of using a vending machine, buy snacks in bulk at warehouse clubs or big-box stores such as Costco, Bulk Barn or Walmart.
- Buy larger containers of snacks at your grocery store.
- Consider moving to healthier snacks: swap almonds, blueberries or mixed raw vegetables for chips and chocolate bars.

Try the change for a month. Track the spending difference and get that cash working for you, instead of the potato chip company.

Hearty Serving

- Two heavy snackers in the family
- Each buys two $2 snacks per day for a total spending, $240 per month
- One quit the snacks, the other started buying in bulk for half the cost
- New cost, two × $1 daily, or $60 monthly
- Savings, $180 monthly

Light Serving

- One light snacker in the family
- Buying one $2 snack per day for a total of $60 monthly
- Switched to buying snacks in bulk at half the cost
- New cost, $30 monthly
- Savings, $30 monthly

Yield

Servings	Monthly Savings	10-Year Value × 173	20-Year Value × 521
Hearty	$180	$31,140	$93,780
Light	$30	$5,190	$15,630
Your info			

Nice savings. As always, make the change and commit the savings right away to debt reduction or increased savings. Imagine the family above increasing their mortgage payment by $180 monthly and saving years of payments. Or investing their snack-based savings and covering a child's entire university education.

Packed Lunch Lyonnaise $ $ $ 🍴 🍴

The pressure was on at the engineering firm where Richard worked. It always felt like there was more to do than time allowed. Right now, a major project was behind for an important client. Each team member had to deliver.

Richard was one of the stars of the company, an organized professional who always delivered. Others often wondered what hidden skills allowed such a high level of continuous performance.

At 11:45 on a Tuesday morning Richard was busy working through a complex set of calculations. He didn't notice his teammates heading out to pick up some lunch at the burger place down the road. By 12:10, he completed the key deliverable and strolled to the kitchen fridge to retrieve the bean and rice salad he had made the night before. He ate at his desk and documented his calculations.

At 12:30, Richard met up with three co-workers for their daily 20-minute walk to clear their minds, get in some fresh air and exercise and prepare for the rest of the day.

By 12:50, Richard was working on the next phase of the project as his teammates sat down to talk TV shows over their burgers and fries, the tell-tale grease seeping through the paper bags.

In just 40 minutes, Richard's smart choices made a big difference. The walk was a fitness improver, the salad was healthier than a burger and the extra time helped with making the deadlines. Leaving the car in the parking lot saved a buck or so in driving costs and another $10 in lunch costs, for a total of $11, or $231 a month. Invested over 10 years that would give Richard an extra $40,000. Small changes, big results.

OK, it's hard to look like a big shooter when you take your lunch to the office. But look again. Once you do the math, you might decide that taking your lunch is the quickest way to actually become a big shooter.

And don't forget the health benefits. When you make your own lunch, you are less likely to eat something loaded with crap, because, well, you made it.

Yes, this one takes a bit of work. But not as much as you think.

Ingredients

- Sunday night, make a big container of salad with your favourite protein on it—a bit of chicken, some beans or tofu. Pack a touch of dressing on the side to mix in at lunchtime. Or make a rice, bean and frozen mixed vegetable combo, ready to microwave. Mix in different sauces for variety—black bean, pasta sauce, red curry or chili powder with lime. Don't forget the after-lunch mints on some of these.

- Try making lasagna or chili, packaging it into lunch portions and taking that to work through the week. Or make two different dishes so you can alternate.

- Invest in the right hardware. Look for salad containers with separate dressing holders and stackable, microwaveable containers that provide all-in-one storage for several types of vittles.

- Buy a re-useable, insulated lunch bag to carry it all in, or kick it old school with a Star Wars lunch box. You know you always wanted one.

Is it all worth it? Let's take a look.

Hearty Serving

- Couple with 16 restaurant lunches and 26 takeout lunches monthly
- Restaurant lunch bill of 16 × $25 = $400, plus takeout lunches of 26 × $10 = $260 for a total cost of $660 monthly
- New lunch cost, 42 × $3 packed lunches = $126
- Savings, $534 monthly

Light Serving

- Single professional
- 21 takeout lunches monthly at $10 each = $210
- New lunch cost, 21 × $3 packed lunches = $63
- Savings, $147 monthly

Yield

Servings	Monthly Savings	10-Year Value × 173	20-Year Value × 521
Hearty	$534	$92,382	$278,214
Light	$147	$25,431	$76,587
Your info			

Looks like the brown bag routine is more appetizing than you thought! It's worth some prep time Sunday nights to add more than a quarter of a million dollars to your retirement fund, don't you think? Or clear out a mortgage several years earlier? Maybe go ahead and dust off that Hello Kitty lunch box after all. Who's laughing now?

Detox Drinks du Jour

$ $ $ 🍸 🍸

Stan and Richard were looking forward to Saturday. It was unusually free of family obligations and house projects. They wanted to start the day with a workout. As they were getting ready, Richard brewed a coffee and poured it into an insulated travel cup. Stan stopped on the way and bought a tall skinny cappuccino.

After a spin class and some weights, they stopped at the mall to pick out a birthday gift for Lucy. Stan was feeling a bit tired from the workout so he grabbed a Diet Coke from the food court. Richard hit a water fountain on the way back to their car.

Lunch was an Asian chopped salad at a local bistro, which Richard washed down with tap water while Stan had another Diet Coke. They then hurried home to jam with Stan's band.

By 6:00 PM, the group was ordering pizza, about half of them opting for soft drinks from the pizza place; the others raided Stan's beer fridge. Things broke up around 9:00, and the guys decided to catch the late show at the movies. Stan stopped at the concession counter for a bucket of popcorn and some root beer, while Richard took his refillable water bottle and found some seats.

That day, Stan spent about $12 more on drinks than Richard. Over the course of 10 years, if invested, that $12 a day could grow to more than $60,000!

Ever notice that when you eat a lot of fast food you crave more of it? The same is true of drinks.

30 days makes a habit. Try skipping the store-bought beverages and fancy café brews.

Ingredients

- Every workplace has fresh, clean water available for free. Get a nice water bottle and keep cool water on hand to replace multiple pops, bottled juices and expensive coffees.
- If your addiction is too powerful, try drinking the coffee provided where you work instead of heading to the coffee shop. I know,

you think it's horrible swill. But try a blindfolded taste test. If the java really is bad, lobby management for upgraded brew.

- Try brewing coffee or tea at home and taking it along in a travel mug. You can't complain about the coffee you made yourself!

Hearty Serving

- Family with two coffee and soft drink devotees
- Each buying two $5 coffees and one $2 soft drinks per day, including weekends
- Total of $24 daily or about $720 monthly
- Switched to drinking company-provided coffee or water at work and using a personal water bottle on the weekend for $0 monthly
- Savings, $720 monthly

Light Serving

- One high-end coffee buyer
- Buying one $5 coffee per day, including weekends, for a total of $150 monthly
- Switched to drinking company coffee at $0 daily on workdays and home brewing Saturday and Sunday at $0.50 daily, for a total cost of $4 monthly
- Savings, $146 monthly

Yield

Servings	Monthly Savings	10-Year Value × 173	20-Year Value × 521
Hearty	$720	$124,560	$375,120
Light	$146	$25,258	$76,066
Your info			

Yes, I did the math right. Many people retire on less than $375,000 and the over-caffeinated family above could do that by changing their daily drinks! Bottoms up!

The Take-Away Container

Food and drink are a big part of our lives and provide much enjoyment, so there is no reason to carve them down to the bone. But we have learned that a few tweaks can make a big difference in our spending, without leaving a bad taste or taking away the fun.

In this section, we looked at 10 ways to save up to $84,251 for our Light Serving and $359,494 for the Hearty Serving over 10 years when invested at 7%:

✓ **Stop paying for water.** Get a personal bottle and fill up for free.

✓ **Go generic.** Step away from the big brands. There is a whole generic world out there, typically 25% cheaper.

✓ **Give yourself some chills.** Consider frozen fruits and vegetables. Less cost, less spoilage and easier to store.

✓ **Cook it yourself.** Shop the perimeter of the grocery store for fresh, whole foods. Learn to peel, chop, cook and save.

✓ **Eat less meat.** Reduce meat consumption for improved health and significant savings.

✓ **Love the sale bin.** Learn to stock up on sale items, particularly non-perishables, to save 25% or more.

✓ **Make a grocery list.** Take a list to the store and avoid purchasing things you already have or don't need.

✓ **Reinvent snacks.** Switch to bulk snacks rather than single-serving ones.

✓ **Pack your lunch.** Some prep time on weekends can set you up with a week's worth of high nutrition at low cost.

✓ **Ditch the drinks.** All that high-end coffee and pop adds up. Make coffee at home or enjoy fresh, clean tap water.

Many of these ideas can become habits with a bit of practice. Be sure to sign up for a loyalty discount card at your grocery store for even more savings—many can be stored on your smartphone.

Household

OK, SO YOU'VE PUT YOUR HOUSING, transportation and food spending on a diet. You've gathered up some savings from the first three sections and used the freed-up cash to pay down some debt or increase your savings rate. That's great progress. But there are lots of interesting recipes still to come.

Savings on household expenditures may seem harder to track down than fresh loquat. Google it; I'll wait. But some simple changes can make a big difference. Use these next 10 recipes to reduce some common household costs and then apply the same thinking to other costs.

Here are some areas we'll look at:

- Personal grooming
- Prescriptions and other drugstore items
- Clothing and dry cleaning
- Fitness expenses
- Day care, kids' activities and higher education

Dry Cleaning Demi-Glace $ ⍩

Bruno was leaving the dry cleaners he had used for years with a stack of shirts in one arm and the dog pulling on his leash on the other.

He met Richard on his way in with an armload of dirty shirts. "I didn't know you used this cleaner," Bruno said. "I'm here every other week and I've never seen you."

"I only come by once a month or so," Richard said.

"You must have a lot of shirts, my friend," Bruno said.

"Not really," Richard replied, "I'm just strategic about them."

"This I need to hear," said Bruno.

Richard explained that while he liked to look crisp and professional at work, the cost of cleaning and pressing his shirts had crept up to $3 per shirt. He realized that his shirts didn't usually get that dirty, just wrinkled.

"So I started buying those no-iron shirts and if I wear a t-shirt underneath, I can wear them twice before I have to have them cleaned. Plus, they look great when I travel for work," Richard explained. "I lowered my dry cleaning bill further since they provide a discount if I pay cash."

The dog was enjoying the fall day and sniffed a few fire hydrants on the way home. Bruno was lost in number-crunching as he walked.

He figured Richard's strategy would save $40 a month. He made the shirt switch and immediately used the savings on cleaning to increase his TFSA contributions by $40 monthly.

All right, what else has been nibbling on your bank balance? The beauty of paying for everything with a debit or credit card is the ability to see all of the expenses at the end of the month. They've got nowhere to hide.

On one hand, dry cleaning bills are likely not the biggest item in your household budget. On the other hand, some simple changes can mean savings with minimal sacrifice. In that way, it's a bit like saving on other boring things like electricity or gas bills.

In most neighbourhoods there are likely two or three dry cleaners. Do some quick price checks. Dry cleaner pricing doesn't change hourly like airplane tickets, so if you compare every couple of years you are likely optimized. Once you have found the price leader, start them off with a couple of shirts to determine quality.

Next, look for ways to reduce your use of dry cleaning.

Ingredients

- For men, wear no-iron shirts with undershirts. This setup means the shirt really doesn't touch your body and looks and smells good for a couple of wearings.
- In a business casual environment, wear golf shirts or sweaters—they tend to be less wrinkly and can be washed at home.
- Hang suits right away and keep the creases lined up on the pants. If the suit isn't actually dirty, take it in to be pressed only, rather than cleaned.
- Women, check labels. Does the item really need dry cleaning? Can it be hand-washed or washed on the gentle cycle and hung to dry?

Another option is to launder your shirts at home. No-iron ones can go straight onto a hanger from the dryer or clothesline and pretty much eliminate your entire dry cleaning bill. If shirts do need ironing, maybe take in some motivational TED Talks as you do the pressing. Enjoy the talk but focus on the iron—keep it moving. Yes, this takes some time but you're saving time not going to the cleaners.

If you don't know how to iron a shirt, your mom probably does. Ask for a lesson.

Hearty Serving

- Two adults
- Spending $100 monthly on dry cleaning
- Switched to lower-cost cleaner
- Switched to no-iron shirts and two wearings per shirt
- Switched to hand- or gentle washing according to the label
- Savings, $30 monthly

Light Serving

- Single professional
- Spending $50 monthly on dry cleaning
- Switched to lower-cost cleaner
- Switched to no-iron shirts and two wearings per shirt
- Savings, $15 monthly

Yield

Servings	Monthly Savings	10-Year Value × 173	20-Year Value × 521
Hearty	$30	$5,190	$15,630
Light	$15	$2,595	$7,815
Your info			

Shaved Blade Roast

Stan loved all kinds of retro things, so for Christmas, Richard got him an old-fashioned double-edge razor, brush, stand and shaving soap. The set reminded Stan of the one his father had when Stan was just a youngster.

He cracked open the soap and loved the woodsy smell. Intrigued, he set off to the bathroom to take the set on its maiden voyage. A few weeks and nicks later, he had learned to use a lighter touch to get a nice, close shave without ending up covered in bits of bloody toilet paper.

He experimented with different blades and began buying them in bulk online once he settled on a favourite. He began adding to his organic soap collection and with a rotation of five, he had enough to keep him shaving for a few years. Stan was amazed that he had eliminated 90% of his shaving costs and as a bonus, was free of the chemicals in aerosol shaving cream.

The other bonus was the waste reduction. Rather than throwing out aerosol cans and entire shaving cartridges, Stan pressed a chipped mug into service to hold the shaving soap and gathered weeks' worth of blades into a tiny box to discard.

It wasn't the most important aspect of his life, but Stan had discovered a luxurious way to shave with lower costs and fewer chemicals on his skin. As the cherry on top, people commented on Stan's pleasant new woodsy scent.

Let's get to work. Pull out a meat mallet and give those shaving cartridges from the drugstore a good whack. Figuratively—we don't want sharp bits of metal flying around. In small packs, cartridges cost about $5 each, which means about $5 weekly or $20 monthly. Then there are those cans of green slop that magically turns into foam. They add up as well—both in cost and in the landfill. And don't look at the list of chemicals that are soaking into your skin. Let's rewrite the shaving recipe.

Ingredients

- Invest in an old-school safety razor and brush.

- Buy the blades online for as little as 12 cents each. They last for about a week.

- Replace the cans of shaving cream with natural shaving soaps—they cost about $10–$15 and last for at least a year. As a bonus, they come in great scents like musk, lime, rum, mint, coconut and almond. Hey—anyone hungry?

- If you want to stay with cartridge blades, try a blade sharpening device like the RazorPit. These devices clean and sharpen your cartridges to make them last longer.

- Another alternative is a web-based shaving club, like Dollar Shave, that ships you razors and soap each month. Costs fall between drugstore cartridge razors and safety razors.

You'll have some upfront costs for a brush, shaving soap and safety razor and a stand to hold it all, a one-time expense of $50–$100, and then you are set for some savings. And a much more enjoyable shaving ritual. The safety razor takes a bit of practice and finesse, but the savings, luxurious feel, healthier ingredients and environmental benefits make it worthwhile.

Hearty Serving

- Family with two shavers
- Using eight cartridges ($40) and one can of shaving cream ($5) per month for a total cost of $45 monthly
- Switched to safety razor, eight blades at $0.12 each and $1 worth of soap each month
- Total cost, $2 monthly
- Savings, $43 monthly

Light Serving

- One shaver
- Using four cartridges ($20) and half a can of shaving cream ($2.50) per month for a total cost of $22.50 monthly
- Switched to safety razor, four blades at $0.12 each and $0.50 worth of soap each month
- Total cost, $1 monthly
- Savings, $21 monthly

Yield

Servings	Monthly Savings	10-Year Value × 173	20-Year Value × 521
Hearty	$43	$7,439	$22,403
Light	$21	$3,633	$10,941
Your info			

OK, not Christmas turkey sized savings, but we are just getting started! And on top of that 22 grand, you'll have fewer chemicals on your skin, a closer shave, a luxurious experience and a lot less garbage heading for the landfill.

Stewed Sports Spending

Vismaya's daughters were avid soccer players and she was pleased at how it was building their confidence and developing them as team players. Many of Vismaya's friends' kids were starting to get into partying, hanging out in malls and discovering too much about...too much. Hopefully her girls would continue their athletic focus.

Compared with other sports, the equipment for soccer was fairly cheap and there were only a couple of team road trips each season. One of the major costs was the program fees. It was a challenge to fit them into her budget.

At a Thursday evening game, Vismaya met Jodi, one of the other parents. Jodi was often cheering exuberantly for her son, Thomas. The two women got to chatting about the high program fees. Jodi mentioned that a friend volunteered to coach her daughter's soccer team and was given a 50% reduction in program fees.

Vismaya approached the soccer coach and he indicated that they needed a team manager to organize the schedule, contact interested parents and help out at games. The role was a volunteer one, but would save Vismaya $600 a year on the cost of having the girls play.

Vismaya signed on and enjoyed the role, meeting other parents and becoming more involved in the game. Rather than spending the freed-up $600, she deposited it into the girls' RESPs, receiving a 20% grant from the government and allowing the resulting $720 to grow sheltered from tax. After one of the games, Vismaya took her daughters as well as Jodi and Thomas out for ice cream to thank Jodi for the idea and to celebrate her success.

Team sports and other activities provide kids with great exercise and a chance to learn about teamwork. But for all the benefits, kids' programs can leave the family budget more than a little overcooked.

Let's look at ways of saving that can work whether your kids are into lacrosse, ski racing, football or dance. Here are some ideas on how to simmer down the cost of the main expenses.

Ingredients

- Buy used equipment to save 40% or more. Remember to check for CSA certification, damage, overuse and expiry dates. Organize a gear swap with friends and neighbours.
- Use early signups to save 10% on tournament and team fees. Consider becoming a team manager or coach for additional savings.
- Carpool to save 50% or more on transportation.
- Buy snacks in bulk. Make meals to pack for road trips to save 30%.
- At tournament time, use travel points, discount hotel sites or Airbnb to save 10% or more.

Consider the overall cost of a sport before signing up for the first time—it's challenging to pull back on a sport once committed. Less gear-intensive sports like soccer are cheaper.

> Don't buy used helmets for sports like hockey, cycling or skiing: it's best to buy new ones so that you are certain the helmet hasn't sustained damage.

Hearty Serving
- Family with three participants in sports or other paid activities
- Total costs equivalent to $125 for equipment and $200 for fees = $325 monthly
- Bought used and/or traded to reduce total equipment cost to $75 monthly
- Registered early to reduce total registration cost to $175 monthly
- New total cost, $250 monthly
- Savings, $75 monthly

Light Serving
- Family with one participant in sports or other paid activities
- Cost equivalent to $42 for equipment and $66 for fees = $108 monthly
- Bought used equipment and/or traded to reduce cost to $25 monthly
- Registered early to reduce registration cost to $58 monthly
- New cost, $83 monthly
- Savings, $25 monthly

Yield

Servings	Monthly Savings	10-Year Value × 173	20-Year Value*
Hearty	$75	$12,975	$25,561
Light	$25	$4,325	$8,520
Your info			

*Assumes 10 years of sports per child. Note that the 20-year value comes from continuing to grow the 10-year value at 7% for another 10 years, but without the monthly savings contributions.

Haircut Mousse with all the Trimmings $ ♥

Once a month, Brad headed to the haircutting place a short stroll from the house for a trim. He had been going to the same place for years.

When Brad first started going to the stylist, he paid about $18 for a cut. More recently, the bill had crept up to more like $42 including the tip. While the cost of the haircut had risen more than 130%, Brad's hair had lost about 50% of its total volume. On a per hair basis, one could say that the cost had risen a hair-raising (sorry) 260%.

In the 1980s, the stylist used scissors and carefully shaped Brad's hair into just the right look. As his pate had thinned, Brad had gone with a shorter look, which worked better with his thin, grey locks. The whole thing was now about a centimetre long, with a bit more on the top.

While at Costco picking up some staples, Lucy spotted a hair clipper set on sale for $45. It even included a cape and some scissors. Since the clippers would pay for themselves with just one saved haircut, Brad agreed to give it a try.

Now, once a month, Lucy covers Brad with the cape, and in 10 minutes the job is done.

Their son, Stan, and his partner, Richard, had just adopted a baby, so Brad and Lucy set up an RESP for the baby's education using the haircut savings.

Invested at 7%, the monthly $42 would grow to more than $7,000 over the next decade. Lucy was keen to find other areas for savings, which left Brad concerned about what the next focus of cuts might be.

Not every personal grooming reduction is as cut-and-dried as Brad's. And it's not easy to break up with your hairdresser since no one else gets your hair and your preferences and knows how to do things just right. That is, until you find yourself travelling and in need of a trim and someone else does it better and cheaper. Maybe it's time to do a little shopping around.

Hairdressers are challenging to research online. It's not like comparison shopping for snow tires or giant jars of mustard. You may want to ask friends and family to see who has a cheap and cheerful (and competent) stylist or salon they recommend.

Even if you end up with a bad referral, any sections where the scalp wasn't scarred will grow back. Eventually.

If you want to cut your hairdressing costs way back, research professional schools near you. Many barbering and hairdressing schools offer free cuts by students. Do you feel lucky?

Ingredients

- Shop for lower-cost haircutting that maintains quality and style.
- Check out hairdressing schools as a low-cost option (if you're brave).
- Offer to pay in cash and see if that lowers the cost.
- Consider doing your own colouring.
- Folks with very short hair: consider switching to clippers and DIY in the back yard. Aim for a breezy day to minimize clean-up.
- Some stylists offer cuts and colour from their homes on their days off. Ask around to see if one of your neighbours has a little haircutting business on the side.

If you have a family, start with one brave soul of each gender to seek out some lower-cost alternatives. If they are able to return to the nest with minimal gouges and no bandages on their ears, take the rest of the family.

Hearty Serving

- Family of five, two adults, three teenagers
- Spending $70 per month for each of two women, $40 for each of three men
- Total, $260 monthly
- Switched to lower-cost salon or barber and paid $50 each for women, $25 each for men
- New total, $175 monthly
- Savings, $85 monthly

Light Serving

- Single person
- Spending $50 monthly
- Switched to lower-cost provider at $25 monthly
- Savings, $25 monthly

Yield

Servings	Monthly Savings	10-Year Value × 173	20-Year Value × 521
Hearty	$85	$14,705	$44,285
Light	$25	$4,325	$13,205
Your info			

A little off the top and more onto the bottom line. It may be time to give your haircut, well, a haircut. This dish pairs nicely with home-based manicure and pedicure savings.

Par-Boiled Prescriptions $ $

Lucy had been concerned about Brad's health. The pain in his knees had been flaring up and it was starting to limit his ability to enjoy some of his favourite activities, including golf and gardening.

Brad had tried a number of natural remedies, including magnetic and copper bracelets. The former had an annoying habit of attracting paperclips and the latter turned his skin green. Neither seemed to alleviate his symptoms.

Finally, Brad saw his doctor, who confirmed that it was, indeed, arthritis and asked whether he had medical coverage. Brad didn't and the doctor winced as he wrote a prescription since the drug was expensive.

Brad stopped to fill the prescription at a pharmacy on the way home, and when he saw the bill, he wasn't sure how he would be able to afford the medication long term. After several days, he found that the medication worked, but he dreaded heading back for the expensive refill.

Jodi suggested he stop by the drugstore up the street, where the pharmacist had always seemed a bit more helpful than most. When it was time for the refill, Brad shared his cost concerns with the young pharmacist when it was time for a refill, and she handed him a pamphlet about a provincial program that subsidizes prescription medication for low-income seniors. She also let him know he was eligible for a senior's discount and gave him the application form for that as well. He completed the forms while he waited for his prescription.

When Brad bragged to his poker buddies about his drugstore savings, they asked whether it might mean more beer and better snacks when he hosted the game.

Brad quietly dealt the cards.

Whether for medication or glasses and contacts, there are lots of ways to over-spend on healthcare. Your eye doctor probably makes more from the frames and lenses he sells than the eye exams. And have you noticed how handy that pharmacy is in the same building as your doctor?

If you don't have a medical plan that covers the cost, or if your plan has an annual limit on your prescription spending, it is always worthwhile to do some comparison shopping.

For medication, be sure your prescription includes the drug identification number (DIN), which is a code for that specific drug at that particular strength. The prescription will also indicate the number of tablets. With this information, you should be able to get prices from other pharmacies. Be sure you discuss cost concerns with both your doctor and the pharmacist. They may be able to offer you some options to temper the costs.

> Some drug companies offer subsidies and discounts for specific medications. Ask your doctor or pharmacist for details.

Ingredients
- Let your doctor know if you don't have medical coverage and always ask for generic drug prescriptions if available.
- Using your prescription information, call the pharmacy section at a couple of drugstores and big-box stores that have pharmacies.
- For glasses, compare pricing at big-box stores such as Costco, along with online services such as Warby Parker, for your next pair. Watch for sales at some of the national eyewear chains— you can often get a second pair of glasses for half price.

If you only occasionally have prescription meds it may not be worth the effort to try to reduce your costs. But if you are on a regular prescription and lack a medical plan, a few phone calls can make a difference of 30–50% on the drugs and even a few dollars on the dispensing fees, which can vary from about $4 to $12.

Hearty Serving
- Family of five with no supplementary medical insurance

- Spending $200 monthly on prescription drugs and the equivalent of $33 monthly on glasses across four eyeglass wearers
- Total costs, $233 monthly
- Bought medication at a warehouse club to reduce cost to $120 monthly
- Bought prescription glasses at a warehouse club to reduce cost to $25 monthly
- New costs, $145 monthly
- Savings, $88 per month

Light Serving

- Single person with no supplementary medical insurance
- Prescription costs of $63 monthly at local drugstore
- Found same prescription for $41 monthly at a warehouse club
- Savings, $22 monthly

Yield

Servings	Monthly Savings	10-Year Value × 173	20-Year Value × 521
Hearty	$88	$15,224	$45,848
Light	$22	$3,806	$11,462
Your info			

Incredible the power of a few phone calls. Once you find the best price, consolidate all your prescriptions with that pharmacy. Bake the freed-up cash into debt reduction or savings!

Trussed and Roasted
Clothing Costs $ $ ♟ ♟

Thomas needed a costume for a Halloween party, so Jodi took him to a local thrift shop to put something together.

Within minutes, they were both laughing as they tried on Nehru jackets from the 60s, tacky Christmas sweaters and feathered hats. Jodi pulled on an old wedding dress over her sweater and pants.

Eventually, they set Thomas up with a classic Canadian "hoser" outfit with old jeans, a red and white toque with matching scarf, a plaid lumberjack shirt and a denim jacket. To complete the look, they added some ear muffs atop the toque and a pair of beat-up work boots. For the party, they could add a back-bacon sandwich and a Tim Hortons coffee cup as props. Thomas texted pictures of his outfit to his friends and he got a few "thumbs up" emojis back.

On the way out, Jodi spotted a beautiful winter coat on the end of a rack. Checking the label, she saw that it was by a well-known designer, and it was even her size. She inspected it thoroughly and it looked like new. Jodi did a quick scan of the store to make sure there was no one there she recognized, then tried the coat on. It was beautiful and the deep navy looked great on her. At $18, it was maybe 5% of the original retail price. Jodi did a quick glance around the store to check for other treasures as they made their way to the cashier.

At first Jodi hid the provenance of the coat from her friends, but after a while she loosened up and openly bragged about it with a laugh. Over time, Bruno, Jodi and the boys would do a monthly trip to the thrift store, smiling at the nostalgia and finding some great bargains.

It's always incredible to find a deal on something great; sure, it's a bit too big/small/boxy but still a pretty good fit. Sort of. And hey, how often do you find *that* label at 40% off?

Six months go by and there it is, forgotten at the back of your closet. The fact is that we wear only about 20% of the clothing we buy. We sell the other 80%, often 10 years later at a yard sale for five cents on the dollar. Or we just give it away. Or we throw it away. So the biggest change to make in this area is to buy only when you really need something and then, only when it is perfect in every respect.

Let's look at this in more detail. Clothing makes up about 6% of a typical Canadian budget. So with a household income of $85,000, about $5,000 is spent on clothes. Twenty percent of these items are worn and 80%, or $4,000 worth, are sold at a yard sale for maybe $200, max, and that's only if you bother having a yard sale. Basically that's burning $3,800 a year. If you bought only the 20% you'll actually wear, and you got all of it used at 10% of its original price, you would spend $100 per year on great clothes that fit. Hmm. Let's scramble our old thinking about buying clothing and start fresh.

Ingredients

- Buy specific items that you need to fill a wardrobe gap.
- Get high-quality clothes with classic styling that fit perfectly.
- Only buy items that really excite you.
- Recycle clothes that don't fit or are out of style.
- Don't shop for the sake of shopping.
- For kids, buy practical or gently used, not designer.
- Check out thrift and consignment shops; you may be surprised at what you find.
- Take a friend shopping or FaceTime one who can talk you out of stupid purchases.
- Keep receipts and leave the tags on until you are absolutely sure you will wear the clothes.

In summary, buy things you love that you will actually wear and that fill genuine holes in your wardrobe, like the brown belt that will liberate your brown shoes from your closet.

Hearty Serving

- Family with two adults and three children

- Spending $400 monthly on clothing
- Reduced the cost of purchased but unworn clothing by buying clothes only when needed, buying quality items that fill a wardrobe gap and carefully checking size and fit
- Shifted some purchases to discount and thrift stores
- Shopped out of season for best pricing
- Savings, $100 monthly

Light Serving

- Single person
- Spending $100 monthly on clothing
- Reduced the cost of buying unneeded clothing
- Savings, $30 monthly

Yield

Servings	Monthly Savings	10-Year Value × 173	20-Year Value × 521
Hearty	$100	$17,300	$52,100
Light	$30	$5,190	$15,630
Your info			

Nice work! Meaningful savings and everything in your wardrobe fits and looks great. Use the savings to clear off that credit card balance left over from the excess clothing you used to buy.

Seared Cell Service $ $ 🍸

Richard and Stan were settling into their new home and money was tight. The occasional unexpected expense, like a car repair or a house issue, would upset their budget, but they were still able to set money aside and hoped to increase their savings rate over time.

One evening Richard's cell phone went missing. He and Stan checked everywhere, to no avail. Richard started to panic; a replacement phone might cost hundreds of dollars.

The next morning, Richard picked up Robin, his carpooling co-worker, who happened to manage the company's telecom support. Richard told Robin about his missing phone. As they drove, Robin reached into the car console looking for the charging port and found... the missing phone. Richard was thrilled and offered to waive Robin's carpooling contribution for the month.

As they pulled into the parking lot, Robin said, "I don't think I've seen your name on the employee discount program we have for phone service with your provider. You could save about $25 a month and you might be eligible for a new phone in case you lose this one for real next time."

Richard signed up for the plan and contacted the bank right away to increase his monthly TFSA contribution by $25.

For most families, the cost of mobile phone service can be daunting. Of course, the original business case for the kids' cell phones was something about how you would be able to stay in touch with them when they are out and about. Although they never miss a Snapchat or a Facebook update from their friends, their devices seem to misfire with incoming messages from the parents. Darn technology!

Cell phone costs are significant but are often overlooked as an area for savings. In most households, there's an ongoing tug-of-war to keep the bills reasonable, the data usage under control and the phone out of the lake, the toilet and the laundry.

While you're not going to stop the gaming and the YouTube consumption entirely, you can put some rules in place to serve up a manageable mobile bill each month. Let's mince some megabytes.

Ingredients

- Get everyone with one provider with the best price plan for your situation.
- See if your company has a program that extends corporate pricing to employees. Such deals may also be offered by professional and alumni associations.
- Have everyone use an app like My Data Manager to track their usage and review the numbers with them.
- Or, better still, could some family members do without cellular data? It means using wi-fi for data, but that can be a serviceable option for many.
- Have your kids pay for their data overages, and if they're working, their whole phone cost, so there is some shared responsibility in the family.
- Ensure everyone has a protective case on their device.
- Invest in a device protection program when you buy new.
- Ensure all the phones are set to use your home wi-fi rather than cellular; same goes for other common locations like schools, offices, airports and gyms.
- Get roaming packages or turn off data when you travel.
- Review your bill carefully each month to spot overspending on data, directory assistance or long distance.
- Call your provider each year to optimize your plan as your needs change—a one-hour call will yield significant savings.
- Use apps like Google Hangouts, Slack, WhatsApp or Facebook Messenger for free wi-fi calling to save on minutes, long distance and roaming charges.

Hearty Serving

- Family with four cell phones and a landline
- Spending $370 monthly
- Set all phones to maximize wi-fi
- Monitored usage with an app
- Called wireless provider to optimize costs
- Moved home phone and internet to cell carrier to get a discount
- New spending, $250 monthly
- Savings, $120 monthly

Light Serving

- Single person, one cell phone
- Spending $75 monthly
- Monitored usage with an app
- Called provider to optimize cost
- New spending, $60 monthly
- Savings, $15 monthly

Yield

Servings	Monthly Savings	10-Year Value × 173	20-Year Value × 521
Hearty	$120	$20,760	$62,520
Light	$15	$2,595	$7,815
Your info			

Season your long-term savings with the newfound cash and serve when you retire.

Lean Ground Learning $ $ $ ♀

During Saturday night dinner, Vismaya's daughter Serena let loose a classic parental nightmare: the untouched school book report due on Monday.

"You're telling me this now?" said Vismaya.

"Well, yah, I just thought of it," shrugged Serena.

"What is the book about?" Vismaya was glaring.

"How would I know? I haven't read it," Serena offered indignantly.

Through clenched teeth, Vismaya said, "you will start reading right after dinner and work on your outline."

"But Mom, I don't have a copy of the book. Can you buy it for me tomorrow?"

Vismaya cleared the dinner plates and sent Serena to find the e-book online. No dice.

The next morning, the bookstore clerk apologized that the title was out of stock and offered to order it. Still seething, Vismaya explained the due date. The clerk smiled and suggested the public library. Vismaya hadn't set foot in a library in 20 years. She recalled old wooden furniture, a musty smell and a lot of "shushing" from the librarian.

What a difference a couple of decades makes, she thought, as she stood in the modern, fresh-smelling library, reading over the list of free resources. Music, digital versions of magazines, community events and guest speakers, all for free. They each got a library card, and Vismaya signed herself up for a computer class.

Serena found the book she needed and her mom checked out some time management reading and assigned that to Serena as a special project.

From cooking to Cantonese to playing the accordion, there are thousands of free and low-cost ways for kids and grown-ups to learn almost anything through books or online learning options at the library.

If you prefer instructor-led classes, Skype and other free communications channels can connect you with some lower-cost options. Or use some of the online options to augment in-person instruction.

Where are you spending money on learning? Let's see if we can skim off some budgetary fat.

Ingredients

- For learning of all kinds, look at online learning sites like Coursera, Udemy and iTunes University.
- For business professional development, consider Lynda.com.
- For musical training, try sites like JustinGuitar.com and Yousician.com.
- For fitness and yoga, YouTube offers channels such as Interval Yoga and Gaia.
- If you want to study a new language, check out free mobile apps like Duolingo.
- For kid's tutoring, try the Khan Academy or YourTeacher apps.
- YouTube offers instruction in everything from building a fence to learning from a top keynote speaker.

Hearty Serving

- Family with two guitar students and one math student
- Two music lessons at $100 each, or $200 monthly; math tutoring at $60 monthly
- Spending $260 monthly
- Switched lessons to JustinGuitar.com, Khan Academy or similar free classes
- Savings, $260 monthly

Light Serving

- Single person
- Taking two business classes for a total of $100 monthly
- Signed up for online learning for a total of $20 monthly
- Savings, $80 monthly

Yield

Servings	Monthly Savings	10-Year Value × 173	20-Year Value × 521
Hearty	$260	$44,980	$135,460
Light	$80	$13,840	$41,680
Your info			

Post-Secondary Pot Roast $ $ $ ♟

Bruno and Jodi's elder son, Ken, was heading to university in the fall. It was time to settle on who would pay for what. Any decision for Ken would set a precedent for when Thomas headed to university.

Ken was a savvy negotiator and wanted to ensure that he set himself up in the best possible financial position. He had worked hard as a landscaper for several summers, but of course, he didn't want to squander his hard-earned cash if his parents would pick up the tab.

But Bruno and Jodi had done some thinking as well and had decided they would cover half the cost of books, tuition, housing and food.

As the negotiations got underway, they found Ken to be very accommodating. He indicated that first-year housing was about half the total cost, so to keep things simple, he proposed that he would cover the housing if his parents would pay for books, tuition and food. Bruno and Jodi smiled at each other, pleased with their responsible young man. They shook on the deal.

As usual, Ken had an ace up his sleeve: he had been accepted as a floor monitor in his dorm, helping other students, managing safety protocols and generally keeping the peace. There was no pay, but the job came with a free room for the year.

Bruno and Jodi weren't sure whether to praise his entrepreneurial spirit or disown him. They grinned and countered with the requirement that Ken drive Thomas to piano lessons for the rest of the summer. Done deal.

So off they go to college or university, babies no longer. And for parents, the void of having no one to nag or drive to soccer practice is filled by an astonishing set of bills, as well as the October 3rd phone call to proclaim they need some additional funds. *Now!*

What to do with the little darlings? Can't leave them to starve and it's challenging to negotiate the tuition bill. You can check for available scholarships (or better still, get the student-to-be to do it). There are savings to be had by buying used books or downloading

PDFs, where legal, but overall, the costs seem fully baked. Or are there some chef's secrets that can help?

Of course, you started saving early, investing conservatively and taking advantage of tax-deferred RESP savings. Beyond that, the key lies in setting expectations up front and not leaving the lid off the spending pot so you don't end up funding some of the, ahem, less-than-academic pursuits.

Ingredients

- Communicate your parental contribution a couple of years before school begins so the student has the time and the focus to start saving their contribution.
- Pay only the hard costs or a percentage of the hard costs (housing, books, tuition, groceries).
- Let your student cover her own beer, residence damage, toga materials, noise complaint tickets, 3:00 AM pizzas and concert tickets.
- Consider paying for only a fixed number of years of schooling. If Junior wants to be a professional student, he can fund it himself.

With this approach, the urgent requests for money are eliminated since the parents' contribution is fixed and known. Your child builds some budgeting and life skills, and you are not providing a bottomless budget of party funds. Win-win. Covering only a fixed number of years helps the student to focus and decide on a major vs. enjoying an open-ended university ticket.

Hearty Serving

- Family expecting a total of 10 years of post-secondary costs (e.g., two children in three-year programs and one in a four-year program spaced so there is one child in school each year)

- Total hard costs, $1,500 monthly (tuition, books, lodging, groceries)
- Plan to cover full costs (hard costs plus any and all extra spending) of $1,833 monthly
- Decided to instead fund only 75% of hard costs of $1,500, or $1,125 monthly
- Savings, $708 monthly

Light Serving

- Family expecting a total of 10 years of post-secondary costs (e.g., two children in three-year programs, and one in a four-year program, spaced so there is one child in school each year)
- Total hard costs, $1,500 monthly
- Plan to cover full costs (hard costs plus extra spending) of $1,833 monthly
- Decided to instead fund only 90% of hard costs of $1,500 monthly, or $1,350 monthly
- Savings, $483 monthly

Yield

Servings	Monthly Savings	10-Year Value × 173	20-Year Value*
Hearty	$708	$122,484	$241,293
Light	$483	$83,559	$164,611
Your info			

*Assumes 10 years of sequential post-secondary attendance across the three children. Note that the 20-year value comes from continuing to grow the 10-year value at 7% for another 10 years, but without the monthly savings contributions.

Deep-Fried Day Care with Blanched Budget $ $ $ ▼ ▼

Stan and Richard brought home their new baby, Melissa. During the first few months, Stan had handled most of the child care, reducing his piano lessons to free up time while Richard continued full time at the engineering firm. Day care costs were high and finances were a challenge, but the guys were thrilled that Stan could care for their baby at home.

Stan was leaning against a deck rail watching Brad and Lucy taking turns holding the baby while he told them about the high cost of licensed day care. There was a loud crack and the deck rail gave way. Stan just managed to catch himself, avoiding the three-metre drop to the garden below.

Once they realized everyone was fine, Brad growled. "Damn fool. I hired that contractor, Frank, to build this deck just two years ago, and it's falling apart!"

They moved to the safety of the living room and discussed what to do about the deck.

Stan pointed out that his drummer, Trevor, had built decks as a summer job during university. Stan was pretty handy, too, and knew his way around power tools. They hatched a plan where Stan and Trevor would rebuild the deck in exchange for Brad and Lucy providing three days of day care for Trevor's toddler and baby Melissa each week for a year.

Stan and Trevor worked on rebuilding the deck every Monday for two months. Finally, it was complete. They all celebrated with a dinner on the new deck, and everyone admired the workmanship.

"Any chance our band could practice up here?" Stan asked with a wink.

"Not until my hearing declines some more," Lucy grinned.

OK, kids are cute, but raising them comes with challenges. As they grow and develop, sharing in their triumphs is incredibly rewarding, from their first steps to their Harvard graduation and that spot on Iron Chef. OK, we can dream!

Some of this unbridled joy gets melted by the costs involved. Day care is doubly challenging, since it is a major expenditure and it usually comes during the early career years when money can be tight and there is a lot of rushing to get the Pablum/vomit/poo cleaned off your clothes as you race out the door at 7:30 AM. Are there ways to trim these costs?

Ingredients

- Consider sharing a nanny with a neighbour, alternating hosting duties every couple of weeks.
- Check your company benefits program for paid parental leave policies and top-up programs.
- Familiarize yourself with parental leave legislation and benefits.
- Do the math to see whether it is better for the lower-income spouse to stay home with the children or to get help.
- Enlist family to help with day care. Can you barter some home improvement labour or other service in return?
- Do some comparison shopping on day care costs. Consider the quality of care, reputation and enrichment in addition to costs.

Hearty Serving

- Family with two working adults and two children
- Spending $2,200 monthly on a private nanny
- Moved to nanny sharing with neighbours, giving nanny a 20% raise
- New day care costs, $1,210 monthly
- Savings, $990 monthly

Light Serving

- Family with two working adults and one child
- Spending $1,100 monthly on day care
- Researched local day care offerings, found an accredited one with great care for $900 monthly
- Savings, $200 monthly

Yield

Servings	Monthly Savings	10-Year Value × 173	20-Year Value*
Hearty	$990	$171,270	$337,402
Light	$200	$34,600	$68,162
Your info			

* Although the child would normally attend school by age 5, many families with both parents working still require child care outside school hours, so assume a total of 10 years of child care. Note that the 20-year value comes from continuing to grow the 10-year value at 7% for another 10 years, but without the monthly savings contributions.

The Take-Away Container

It's easy to overlook the everyday ways we can slice a little spending here and dice a few costs there. This section offered up 10 areas that can save a potential total of $158,468 for our Light Serving and a whopping $432,327 for the Hearty Serving over 10 years, when invested at 7%. Not bad for expenses most of us assume are fixed.

✓ **Get lean with the dry clean.** Find a cheaper dry cleaner and use no-iron shirts and washable clothes.

✓ **Shave like grandpa.** Swap expensive cartridge razors and aerosol creams for safety razors and shaving soap.

✓ **Get creative with the kid stuff.** Find savings in activity fees, team travel, snacks and equipment.

✓ **Trim the trimming.** Look for a lower-cost hairstylist, pay cash for a discount and try doing some trimming at home.

✓ **Prescribe yourself some lower drug costs.** Ask about generic medications, shop around to find a helpful pharmacy and look for seniors' and other discounts.

✓ **Stop throwing away money on clothes.** Buy a few pieces you love and truly need, and don't snack on unneeded items at the mall.

✓ **Get serious with your mobile.** Optimize wireless plans, use free services, protect devices from damage and serve up data family style so everyone can share responsibly.

✓ **Learn to learn in new ways.** Consider online and app-based learning versus in-person. Explore the free resources at the public library.

✓ **Lower the cost of higher education.** Pay some of the hard, set costs while your kids pay the variable costs.

✓ **Mind the cost of minding the kids.** Barter with other parents, share nannies, shop around for low-cost care.

Most household costs are great candidates for some creative cookery. Look for anything that can be negotiated, shared, reduced or found for free. Continue to scour household expenses and free up cash for debt reduction and investing for financial freedom. Check out the Ingredients section at CashflowCookbook.com for tested products and services that can help.

Lifestyle

AFTER YOU'VE PAID FOR INSURANCE, taxes, oil changes and electricity bills, who knows? Maybe you'd like to have some fun as well. Part of the bonus of saving on things like groceries and the gas bill is that you can spend some of your savings on things that are actually enjoyable.

Here in the Lifestyle section, we will look at some things that people enjoy (for better or worse):

- Music
- Books, magazines, newspapers
- Vacations
- Fitness
- Drinking
- Smoking
- Casinos and lottery tickets
- And more!

As always, feel free to skip the recipes that don't apply to you and to use your own assumptions for the savings math. Be sure to get full value from the monthly savings by paying down debt or increasing your savings rate. Don't just let the savings sink into the stew of your chequing account.

Music Mincemeat

Bruno sat at the kitchen table and stared at his laptop while Thomas noisily made a sandwich behind him.

"What are you doing, Dad?" he asked, the jam-spreading knife leaving a red trail as it gathered peanut butter from the jar.

"I'm buying music for our dinner party tonight," Bruno replied.

"Ah, first of all, why are you buying music? Lame. Second," the boy added as he looked over his father's shoulder, "you need some fresh tunes."

"Look, I don't want to do anything illegal, and what fresh tunes do you have in mind?"

"It's totally legal: check out the music channels on YouTube, subscribe to some cool ones and you're good. Like Suicide Sheep or Eton Messy."

"Suicide Sheep? Good lord!"

Thomas took over his dad's keyboard, his fingers tapping at twice the speed of his old man's. In short order, Bruno had multiple YouTube music channels on his laptop and a lot of peanut butter and jam on the keyboard.

Thomas grabbed his PB&J and sprinted up to his room to do homework. Bruno listened to one of the YouTube channels, closed his eyes and was loving the music.

Jodi arrived home and hauled three big bags into the kitchen.

"I've been out shopping for the party and you're sitting there listening to music? And look at the mess you left!"

Bruno took the heat for the sandwich mess as his way of thanking Thomas and quickly set the table for the party.

Music is soul tingling. It lifts the spirits and stimulates the mind. It can drain the bank account with subscription and single-song download charges. You may be paying too many notes for your notes. So crank it up, but let's put the costs in the deep freeze.

Although recorded music sales are down, streaming and downloading are on the rise. Pull some credit card statements and see what your household has been spending on music. Hmm. Lots of zesty expenditures.

Ingredients

- For vinyl, get to know used record stores in your area, swap with friends, check yard sales and look at online sites like Discovery-Records.com.

- For instruments, look at Kijiji and Craigslist for used kit at about half the cost of new. Set up alerts for exactly what you need so you are pinged when that maple-neck American Standard Stratocaster (with whammy bar) comes up for sale.

- Most music stores stock used instruments and gear, often reconditioned and with warranties.

- For streaming, consolidate multiple streaming accounts into one family sharing account, such as Apple Music or Spotify.

- Try free apps like Jango or Slacker Radio. Some play music to suit your mood, time of day or musical preference. Others have light versions (with advertising) and premium (without).

Hearty Serving

- Family with two parents and three children
- Spending $20 monthly on single songs
- Two members on Spotify for a total of $20 monthly
- Two members subscribe to Apple Music for a total of $20 monthly
- Moved everyone to Apple Music Family Sharing for $15 monthly
- Savings, $45 monthly

Light Serving

- Single person
- Spending $20 monthly on single songs
- Got free Spotify offer from wireless carrier for $0
- Savings, $20 monthly

Yield

Servings	Monthly Savings	10-Year Value × 173	20-Year Value × 521
Hearty	$45	$7,785	$23,445
Light	$20	$3,460	$10,420
Your info			

Thirty minutes of assessing, some quick tuning and voilà, wealth through music. Be sure to lock away the benefits in debt reduction or savings.

Reading Ravioli $

Lucy was proud of her penny-pinching prowess when it came to groceries. Thanks to buying in bulk, watching for sales, making good use of the freezer and choosing generic brands, she could feed herself and Brad a variety of healthy, balanced meals for about $120 a week. But that still took the monthly total over $500, making groceries a focus item on their fixed retirement income.

One Saturday, as she chatted with the cashier at the supermarket, she grabbed her usual magazines and tossed them on the belt. As Lucy packed the bags, the cashier said, "That's $142.68." Lucy was astonished. How could three bags of groceries possibly cost that much?

"That seems high," she replied. "Did something scan twice?" The cashier scrolled through the items on the screen. A group of items stood out at the bottom of the list. "I think it's the magazines," the cashier smiled. "They sure do add up. Personally, I read mine on my iPad. You want to put one back?" she asked, indicating the most expensive, at nearly $10.

Embarrassed, Lucy said no, paid and left.

As she unpacked her bags at home, she wondered how she could she have missed noticing the cost of the magazines. Maybe the prices, printed in tiny type on the corner, maybe just years of habit, but a bit of math revealed that at $5 or $6 or more per magazine, her reading materials were actually consuming about 13% of their "grocery" spending.

A quick search on her iPad revealed several magazine apps, including one that gave her unlimited reading for just $12 per month, including most of her favourite publications. "No brainer," she smiled as she subscribed.

Lucy wondered if her other reading materials were taking too big a bite out of their budget. She remembered her yoga friend, Vismaya, mentioning getting a library card. Who knew? She found the library website and discovered she could download e-books, reserve new releases and yes, read magazines, all online.

Reading materials aren't that big a spending category for most of us—really just a daily newspaper, maybe a paperback for the trip to the beach, perhaps something trashy from the grocery checkout.

Don't forget this month's book club selection and the kids' textbooks. And a few self-help books to gather dust on a home-office desk. Hmm. Maybe that *is* a substantial meal. Grab the salad bowl and let's toss around some better ways to read.

Ingredients

- Switch to digital versions of the newspapers you read. They're always on time, never arrive wet and are often cheaper. A bonus is the lighter recycling bin each week.
- Try mobile sites and apps like Flipboard and Reddit to build your personalized digital reading source. For free.
- Order digital tablet versions of the books you want. They're cheaper, download instantly and don't come with traffic or parking hassles.
- Look for used books at garage sales and on Amazon, usually selling for 10–50% of the cost of new books.
- Buy used textbooks for your kids. Sell the old ones.
- For magazines, look at the magazine apps, such as Texture, which provide dozens of titles for the cost of a single newsstand issue.
- And here is a crazy one: public libraries are still a thing! Today they offer digital books, magazines, online learning, book readings and music. Free.

Hearty Serving

- Family with two parents and two children
- Newspaper subscription for $45 monthly, four magazine subscriptions and 20 single issues per year for the equivalent of $26 monthly and new textbooks for the equivalent of $58 monthly
- Total spending, $129 monthly
- Switched to a news app, cancelled newspaper delivery, saving $45 monthly

- Used a magazine app for $10 monthly, saving $16 monthly
- Bought used textbooks for $35 monthly, saving $23 monthly
- Savings, $84 monthly

Light Serving

- Single person
- Buying single magazine issues for $10 monthly and paperbacks for $20 monthly, for a total of $30 monthly
- Eliminated grocery store magazines, read trash online on free sites like Buzzfeed.com, saving $10 monthly
- Switched from new paperbacks to yard sale books for $2 monthly, saving $18 monthly
- Savings, $28 monthly

Yield

Servings	Monthly Savings	10-Year Value × 173	20-Year Value × 521
Hearty	$84	$14,532	$43,764
Light	$28	$4,844	$14,588
Your info			

Some of these ideas require rethinking old habits, but the savings are delicious little treats.

Diced Salsa with Chips $ $ 🍸

Brad was in line at the corner store, juggling a carton of milk and three tins of tuna while the gent in front of him carefully picked his lottery tickets, checking the numbers against a well-worn scrap of paper.

"Oh wait! Sorry, I need that other one just to the right. The one with the eights in it."

"Seriously?" thought Brad as he rebalanced his milk and tuna. As the man turned, Brad recognized him as Frank, a contractor who had botched some repairs at Brad's house.

The transaction was finally over and Frank paid for his tickets. "Oh wait!" said Frank again, "I need you to check a couple of old tickets here." He dug them from his pocket. The ticket machine blazed to life with lights and bells—and played the happy song.

"Looks like you're up a grand!" said the clerk.

"Wow! Can you believe that! My first real win! A thousand bucks! It's like money from the stars!"

Brad elbowed his way to the counter and set his milk and tuna down noisily. "How long you been playing?" he asked, unsmiling.

"Well, I guess about 20 bucks worth each week for the last couple of years."

"Looks like the money didn't come from the stars after all." Brad shook his head.

It's hard not to get seduced by that $41 million lottery jackpot, the slot machine that is just starting to heat up or that last...wait...second last, poker game. The yacht, private jet and secluded beach are oh-so-close; there can be no quitting now.

As promising as it sounds, the odds of winning a major jackpot are about 10 million to one. A venomous snake bite, being hit by lightning or being kidnapped by radicals are all much more likely, although admittedly less desirable.

So, while the Canadian gambling industry does very well, with annual revenue of about $13 billion, the general idea is for the house to keep most of the money. In short, unless you own the casino or are running the lottery, gambling is not a great wealth plan. But shockingly, 34% of Canadians plan on using lottery winnings to fund their retirement.[9]

The average Canadian adult spends $534 annually on gambling[10]; men living alone spend 50% more than women.[11] Looks like too many of us are broiling our savings on a blackjack barbecue.

Ingredients

- If you are addicted to gambling and have built up gambling debts, now is the time to get professional help.
- If you are in control, but are in the habit of regularly buying lottery tickets, consider committing the same amount of money to debt payments or savings instead.
- If a night or a weekend at the casino with your besties is a regular thing, see if you can make that a hike or a spa day instead. Or switch the venue to each other's homes and play poker for quarters.

For simplicity's sake in the examples below, we will assume annual spending of $534 per person and will ignore the value of smaller prizes that may be won from time to time.

---

[9] BMO poll, Jan. 30, 2014.
[10] Institute of Marriage and Family Canada.
[11] Statistics Canada.

Hearty Serving

- Two gamblers in the household
- Each gambles $45 monthly
- Eliminated gambling entirely
- Savings, $90 monthly

Light Serving

- Single person
- Gambles $45 monthly
- Eliminated gambling entirely
- Savings, $45 monthly

Yield

Servings	Monthly Savings	10-Year Value × 173	20-Year Value × 521
Hearty	$90	$15,570	$46,890
Light	$45	$7,785	$23,445
Your info			

If your gambling is fun, modest and under control and you consider it an entertainment expense, no problem. If you are carrying debts and still spending on lottery tickets, you may want to redirect that money to paying what you owe. If you are counting on gambling as part of your retirement fund and your expense is above the national average, you may need to rethink your strategy.

Night Out à la Mode $ $ ¶

Thursday night was date night for Bruno and Jodi, and for years they had gone to the movies, indulging in greasy popcorn washed down with 28 ounces of fizzing sugar. It wasn't doing their waistlines any favours, but it was a nice tradition.

One night in December, Bruno met Jodi for their date after her school board meeting. They jumped on the subway with no particular movie in mind.

As they strolled hand in hand, enjoying the festive lights and the tingle of fresh snow on their faces, they paused to look at the displays in the art gallery window. Neither had set foot inside for decades. Their eyes met and they shared an unspoken "let's check it out."

Jodi pulled out her wallet at the admissions counter but the clerk pointed to the "Free on Thursday" sign. Bonus! They started in the Canadian gallery and learned about colour, style and meaning as used by artists they'd barely heard of. They shared their reactions to the canvases and their ideas about what would work in their house. At 7:30, they attended a session by a cellist who shared her compositions, the inspiration for her pieces and her journey to become a soloist.

As they walked back to the subway hours later, they realized they had forgotten about dinner. They found a hole-in-the-wall café and discussed the art and music over a low-cost meal. Jodi pulled out her phone and they started a list of other fun, low-cost, healthy date night ideas, including the museum, concerts in the park, pay-what-you-can night at the local theatre and Groupon cooking classes.

The bill came and Jodi slid it to Bruno. He raised an eyebrow. "I got the art gallery," she smiled.

Savings don't show up only in mundane areas like car insurance, gas bills and groceries. Here's a delectable easy-to-execute recipe for budget entertainment.

Ingredients

- For high-end live entertainment consider the savings of subscriptions vs. individual tickets, or look for Groupon.com deals.

- For concerts, check for tickets on Kijiji, but be careful of scams.
- Try BrownPaperTickets.com for reasonably priced local music, theatre and comedy, or watch for pay-by-donation nights and free preview performances.
- Most movie theatre chains have a "cheap night," and cinema loyalty points programs can save cash on admission and snacks.
- For attractions, look at local sites like CityPass.com and provincial sites like AttractionsOntario.ca for coupons.
- Do an online search for the name of the attraction you're interested in and "coupons" before booking online. You might find a deal.
- Check with Costco or other membership retailers to see if they offer discount vouchers.
- Check with your employer, alumni association and automobile association for discounted tickets for events and attractions.

Hearty Serving
- Family of five
- Seeing five high-end theatre shows a year, two tickets at $130 each, for the equivalent of $108 monthly
- Visiting family attractions (amusement parks, water parks, etc.) five times a year, for the equivalent of $125 monthly
- Bought theatre tickets to less-expensive shows at BrownPaper-Tickets.com for $25 each, totalling $21 monthly
- Used Groupon passes to save 25% on family attractions, for $94 monthly
- New cost, $115 monthly
- Savings, $118 monthly

Light Serving
- Single person

- Seeing five sporting events and five ballets each year averaging $75 per ticket, for the equivalent of $63 monthly
- Switched to employer discounted sporting event tickets at 20% off for a new cost of $25 monthly
- Switched to half-price rush ballet tickets at $37 each or $15 monthly
- New cost, $40 monthly
- Savings, $23 monthly

Yield

Servings	Monthly Savings	10-Year Value × 173	20-Year Value × 521
Hearty	$118	$20,414	$61,478
Light	$23	$3,979	$11,983
Your info			

Numerous online resources can help you save on live music, theatre and attractions. Take the time to bookmark some useful ones for your location. Enjoy the events and savour the cashflow benefits too.

Julienne of Gym Costs in a
Light Sweat Sauce

$ $ $ ⓨ

On Saturday mornings Richard and Stan woke up early and drove out to their gym near their former residence. After a big workout, they would clean up and drive back to meet their neighbours Kris and Lee for brunch at a café near their new home.

That Saturday, traffic was nasty driving back from the gym. Stan texted their friends to let them know they would be late. They inched along the street. The stress was palpable in the car.

Forty minutes late, they slipped into a parking space. As they parked, Richard noticed a fitness club just up the block. He must have walked by it hundreds of times without a second look. While Stan fed the parking meter, Richard snapped a photo of the club to remind him to check it out on the internet.

At brunch, Richard asked Kris and Lee about the neighbourhood gym—it turned out they were members! The rates were $30 less a month than the gym on the other side of town. "No more 'up at 6, quick coffee, on the road to the gym by 7,'" noted Richard.

"And no more driving all the way out to our old place," added Stan. "There's something absurd about driving to the gym, spending 40 minutes on the treadmill, and then driving back home."

"And no more being 40 minutes late for brunch," said Lee in a mock reprimand.

Well, you didn't end up looking as good as the airbrushed, spray-tanned model on the poster at the fitness club that convinced you to get the three-month-free, act-now-cancel-any-time membership. Dang.

But the memory lingers, as does the pre-authorized payment that still works out with your bank account each month. In a family, there may be two or three of these phantom gym memberships. Perhaps no one even knows who is still a member where.

Nothing wrong with fitness, or great gyms, as long as people are using the memberships. Let's get out the blender and liquefy these wasted costs.

Ingredients

- Inventory your family fitness memberships. Who is using what? Can any be eliminated?
- Shop around for lower-cost gyms in your area with similar facilities.
- Check out your local community centre or YMCA for low-cost or free classes, swimming or other activities.
- Check your work benefits for a gym subsidy or discount program.
- Can you do away with some of the gym memberships and exercise another way?
  - Search YouTube for bodyweight exercise programs. Who knew you've been carrying your own gym with you all along?
  - Hit the yard sales or Craigslist and buy some fitness equipment for your home.
  - Take up running or biking for some nearly free cardio workouts.

Hearty Serving

- Family with two adults and three teens
- Spending $300 monthly on gym memberships
- Discovered an unused employer gym subsidy of $50 monthly
- Eliminated one unused membership of $50 monthly
- Switched to a cheaper gym for one membership, saving $30 monthly
- Total savings, $130 monthly

Light Serving

- Single person
- Spending $100 monthly on an unused gym membership
- Cancelled membership, joined running club and switched to YouTube-led, home-based bodyweight exercises
- Now spending $40 monthly on running shoes and clothing
- Savings, $60 monthly

Yield

Servings	Monthly Savings	10-Year Value × 173	20-Year Value × 521
Hearty	$130	$22,490	$67,730
Light	$60	$10,380	$31,260
Your info			

Video Vichyssoise $ $ $ 🍸 🍸

Brad and Lucy looked forward to settling in to watch TV together. Ever since Stan had given them a device to connect their TV to the internet, they'd spent a lot of time binging science documentaries on Netflix or watching TED Talks. It sure beat flipping channels only to find nothing worth watching.

Brad texted Stan to thank him for the device and for showing them how to use it.

Stan: More than welcome,
glad you and Mom are enjoying it.

Brad: We love it. Just hate paying that TV company bill for shows we never watch.

Stan: You don't need cable anymore to use that device.

Brad: You could have mentioned that sooner!

Stan: Call them now!

Brad knew the drill with the cable company. He dialed, put his phone on speaker and set to work on one of his Mallard decoys. He had completed carving the head and most of the neck when the call centre rep answered. After three can-I-put-you-on-a-short-hold's, he had most of the body roughed out and his service was cancelled.

Brad and Lucy decided to use the savings for a great dinner out each month. Their finances were in great shape and it was time to enjoy some of their diligence.

The chronology is a blur. From black and white to colour, from rabbit ears to cable, to lugging home the VHS machine and some videos (be kind—rewind! Yeah, right), to Netflix shipping discs in the mail (how could that work?), to Netflix streaming (really worked) to Apple TV, Roku, Slingbox and Chromecast. And even better, digital rabbit ears.

With all of this change, who has time to bake in the lowest costs? You do! Go look at a copy of your TV content bills. Take an hour to figure out what you are paying for and who in the house watches what. Odds are someone added a channel package to catch some show that was cancelled three seasons ago. Time to ladle out some savings.

Ingredients

- Consider cutting the TV cord entirely. Yes, I know you will miss the ads, infomercials, upcoming show previews and the reality series about hoarding.

- Switch to the new skinny TV bundles for a light fix of basic cable and local content.

- Look at Apple TV for free content, podcasts, TED Talks and paid movies.

- Try Netflix, Amazon or Hulu for all-you-can-eat TV shows and movies. Once you get used to being able to binge watch episodes, it is hard to go back to one-episode-at-a-time, commercial-laden TV.

- Explore devices like Chromecast or Roku for access to movies, music, content and more from your TV.

- If you travel a lot or have a vacation property, have a look at Slingbox. A low, one-time fee lets you watch everything available on your home TV, anywhere in the world and from any device with an internet connection, saving you that second cable subscription.

- Sports can be a challenge. If you follow only one or two sports, you can order coverage from the NBA or NFL, for example, directly and use one of the methods above.

- Install a digital antenna if you're in an area with strong over-the-air coverage. This is also a great solution for sports access. Go to TVFool.com to check for signal strengths and available channels at your address.

Hearty Serving

- Two properties
- Two full cable subscriptions at $100 for a total of $200 monthly
- Moved to a digital antenna* for city home for $0 monthly
- Moved to Apple TV and Netflix** at vacation property for $10 monthly + four videos monthly at $12 for a total of $58 monthly
- Savings, $142 monthly

Light Serving

- One home
- One cable subscription at $100 monthly
- Moved to Netflix and small in-house antenna* for $10 monthly
- Savings, $90 monthly

Yield

Servings	Monthly Savings	10-Year Value × 173	20-Year Value × 521
Hearty	$142	$24,566	$73,982
Light	$90	$15,570	$46,890
Your info			

* Yes, there is a cost for a digital antenna, about $300 for a large outside one and $100 or less for an in-home model. Feel free to deduct the cost from the 10- and 20-year savings!

** Netflix can be used in more than one location and multi-user licences are available—check the latest offerings. The extra data use can lead to internet overage charges, so you may need to up-size your internet plan, reducing savings somewhat.

Travel Bill Tostada $ $ $ 🍴 🍴

Vismaya was pleased with herself. In the two years since she'd divorced Frank, she had toasted two large credit card balances, mixed up a tasty balance in a family RESP and served up some home fix-it jobs herself.

Slicing about $1,000 a month from their spending had given the family some financial freedom. It was time to reward herself and the girls with a great vacation, maybe someplace warm.

After two hours online, she had found a great hotel, cheap flights and even attractions that the girls would enjoy. She was about to book it when her eldest, Caroline, walked in.

Caroline loved the idea of a trip but wanted a hotel with a gym. They found a nicer hotel, still close to the beach and with a great gym for about the same price, but Caroline pointed out that the flight out conflicted with her last exam. More searching and sorting and finally they had a great itinerary.

Vismaya thought she had better get input from her younger daughter— she was sure to have an opinion and was due home any minute. Serena arrived, dropped her knapsack in the middle of the hallway and her purse in front of the bathroom door. Vismaya was halfway through telling her about the trip to Florida and all the fun they would have when Serena gave her the mother of all eye-rolls.

"The Canadian dollar has dropped 30% against the American, we're tight on money and you geniuses want to go to Florida? Why not take advantage of the plunging peso and go to Mexico?"

Darn it! Vismaya hated it when Serena was right. But the logic was sound. The three of them gathered around the laptop buzzing with excitement about the hotels and attractions in Guadalajara.

If you are in the habit of enjoying a nice annual vacation that adds to your debt load and sinks you deeper in the hole, you may want to do some "staycations" for a year or two while getting your finances in order, free up some cashflow and clear out some debt. By following some of the other recipes you will be able to build a solid financial base and make vacations fun and affordable.

If you can enjoy a regular vacation while continuing to grow your net worth each year, then by all means continue to do so. But let's see if we can plate up some ways to do it more economically, without taking away any of the fun.

Ingredients

- Use one travel rewards card for all work and personal spending to build a decent travel points balance.
- Look at Airbnb, TripAdvisor and Trivago to find independent hotels and Hotels.com, Priceline and Hotwire for the best deals on the majors.
- Choose midweek flights rather than weekends and book well in advance.
- Travel just outside peak season (i.e., shoulder season) for your destination. If you are flexible, look at last-minute travel sites like LastMinute.com.
- Check for free shuttles from airports to hotels and the city centre rather than paying for cabs.
- Buy some basic groceries to keep in your hotel room fridge to save on eating out for every meal and snack, or consider renting a condo or choosing a hotel with a kitchen so you can make most of your own meals.

Hearty Serving

- Family of five, annual vacation
- Spending equivalent of $858 monthly for air and lodging
- Flew midweek to bring air tickets from equivalent of $625 monthly to $525
- Booked Airbnb apartment to take lodging from equivalent of $233 monthly to $133

- Used travel reward points to reduce cost by equivalent of $50 monthly
- New cost, $608 monthly
- Savings, $250 monthly

Light Serving

- Single person, annual vacation
- Buying one-week all-inclusive package for equivalent of $258 monthly
- Moved trip to shoulder season and paid equivalent of $208 monthly
- Used travel reward points to reduce cost by equivalent of $25 monthly
- New cost, $183 monthly
- Savings, $75 monthly

Yield

Servings	Monthly Savings	10-Year Value × 173	20-Year Value × 521
Hearty	$250	$43,250	$130,250
Light	$75	$12,975	$39,075
Your info			

There are many, many more ways to save on travel and dozens of apps and websites that can help. Check out the Ingredients section at CashflowCookbook.com for new ideas. Stay curious, research each component (air, car, lodging), add new techniques and flavours and immediately use the savings to reduce debt or add to your nest egg.

Time-Off Trappings Tofu $ $ $ 🍸 🍸

Bruno was running late to meet up with his buddy Glen for a beer at the neighbourhood sports bar. It was a crisp winter night and the snow squeaked underfoot. He arrived at the bar and found Glen halfway through a beer in a booth by the window. Condensation dripped down the panes as Bruno removed his coat and ordered his first beer. Glen seized the opportunity to order his second while griping about the weather.

They divided their attention between the hockey game on TV and getting caught up on the business world and their families. The two enjoyed sharing life hacks and ideas for side hustles. They had a lot in common but Glen was a passionate cottager and golfer while Bruno was more of a skier and road biker. Bruno was a Leafs fan while Glen was devoted to the Habs.

"You will love this," Glen began.

"You started a fashion blog?" Bruno offered.

"No. No I did not. I used Airbnb to rent out my cottage—got $5,500 for the season! Finally dawned on me that we never go up there in the winter and it is a 20-minute drive to that ski resort." Glen was beaming.

"A pioneer in the sharing economy," laughed Bruno as they clinked their glasses.

Over the course of the evening, Glen described some upgrades he planned to make to the cottage. The game ended, they paid the bill and then headed out into the winter night.

Bruno pulled his toque over his ears as he trudged home in the snow. He marveled at Glen's inventiveness and how he always had an angle on things. Then it hit him: his ski cabin sat unused all summer and was close to a lake with some great fishing areas.

The cold bit at his bare fingers as he navigated the Airbnb site on his smartphone, squinting through his foggy reading glasses as he checked local rental rates.

OK so you absolutely had to own that cottage/scooter/snowmobile/hobby tractor/sailboat/chalet/ski boat/sports car. But as you look at your finances, you realize the debt would shrink or the savings would grow much quicker without the taxes, loan payments, insurance, maintenance and repair costs being funnelled to your toys.

But on the other hand...dang, it's hard to part with them once you have them! Is there a way to have all the fun with fewer calories?

Ingredients

- If the questionable item is one you could share, why not sell a half interest to a friend? Set up a shared calendar on your smartphones for bookings. Share the work, maintenance and insurance and apply this bit of new income to your debts or savings.
- Could you rent your item to others? Or could you sell it and just rent one when you really need it?
- Could you downsize the item? Sell the big one and get a smaller one on Kijiji or Craigslist. Set up an alert so you know when the right one comes along. Research quality and ownership cost on *Consumer Reports* online.
- Cut the repair costs by getting the repair manual, viewing YouTube videos or partnering with a technically minded friend to learn how to do the maintenance yourself.
- Shop the insurance. Double check that you aren't paying twice for the coverage.
- For equipment you will use infrequently, like that tractor you were sure you needed, see if you can rent it from a building supply or tool rental shop.

- If you sell an asset, immediately put the proceeds in your savings pantry or toward paying off debt.
- Be sure to draw up a clear agreement between the partners if you sell an interest in or rent out your asset.

Hearty Serving

- Family owns a sailboat valued at $40,000
- Use boat only some weekends
- Sold a 50% interest for $20,000*

- Saved half the cost of insurance, $67 monthly
- Saved half the cost of dock rental, $67 monthly
- Saved half the cost of maintenance and sails, $166 monthly
- Savings, $300 monthly

Light Serving

- Family owns an older sports car valued at $20,000
- Use car lightly
- Sold the car for $20,000
- Saved $125 on insurance, $83 on maintenance and $50 parking and storage monthly
- Cost savings, $258 monthly
- Rented a convertible for three weekends for equivalent of $50 monthly
- Savings, $208 monthly

Yield

Servings	Monthly Savings	10-Year Value** × 173	20-Year Value** × 521
Hearty	$300	$51,900	$156,300
Light	$208	$35,984	$108,368
Your info			

* Value of debt paydown or savings contribution from selling a toy and value of depreciation savings not included in yield table.

** Assumes the arrangement would continue for 10 or 20 years

Char-Broiled Restaurant Cheques

$ $ $ ♔ ♔

Once a month Bruno and Jodi met up with their friends Glen, Kim, Jim and Laura to enjoy dinner at a local restaurant. The guys tended to congregate at one end of the table while the ladies shifted to the other. It was togetherness and separateness at the same time, with each group deep in its own conversation.

"Is this place Szechuan? Hopefully it's not too spicy," said Jodi as they drove to the restaurant.

"Well the bill was a bit spicy at that last place. Those guys sure like the expensive food."

Meanwhile, Glen and Kim were carpooling with Jim and Laura.

"I love these dinners!" said Glen.

"Yep, Bruno and Jodi are a laugh. But should we have picked a spicy place? Not sure Jodi likes that," said Kim.

"Good thing we carpooled. Seems like we keep finding more and more expensive restaurants," said Jim, ever the frugal banker.

"It's Bruno and Jodi—they like the high-end places," said Laura.

They met in the entry and were seated at a table by the window, which has pros and cons on a winter night in Canada. But there was a big gas fireplace in the centre of the room so it was cozy. They looked at their menus. The entrées started at $55 and the wine list featured very little south of $150. Most of the dishes had three or four chili pepper icons.

"Hmm, for futures...should we maybe set a price limit on these dinners?" said Bruno.

"Price limit? I thought you guys liked the fancy places," said Glen. Everyone exchanged looks around the table, then laughed.

"So we all wanted to find more reasonable places but didn't because we thought the others were food snobs? I need a glass of Merlot," said Jim.

There is nothing like a sunny day on a patio with good friends, great food and perhaps a jug of beer. And few things can beat a romantic dinner in a beautiful restaurant.

But if you are steeped in credit card debt and your statements look like a bar and restaurant guide, it may be time for some adjustments. Let's not take the fun out of everything, but a little fine-tuning on ordering and frequency will chill your bill.

Let's look at a "fully loaded" restaurant bill.

Menu Item	Item Cost	Tax (13%)	Tip (15%)	Total Cost	Cost for 2 Diners Fully Loaded	New
Bottled water	$6	$0.78	$0.90	$7.68	$15.36	$0
Cocktail	10	1.30	1.50	12.80	25.60	0
Appetizer	12	1.56	1.80	15.36	30.72	30.72
Wine, 2 glasses	12	1.56	1.80	15.36	30.72	30.72
Entrée	26	3.38	3.90	33.28	66.56	66.56
Dessert	12	1.56	1.80	15.36	30.72	15.36
Total	$78	$10.14	$11.70	$99.84	$199.68	$143.36

Ingredients

- Skip the opening cocktail to save calories, liver damage, potential impaired driving charges—oh yeah, and money!
- Split a dessert to save both the cash and the paunch.
- Reduce dining out frequency and get into gourmet home cooking.

> Stop paying for water in restaurants. Tap water is perfectly good, less wasteful and a lot less expensive than fizzy water from the Alps.

Hearty Serving

- Family of five
- Dining out four times per month for a total cost of $800
- Switched to two dinners out per month with tap water, no soft drinks, no appetizers and no desserts for a total of $325 monthly

- Savings, $475 monthly

Light Serving

- A couple
- Dining out three times per month for a total cost of $600
- Maintained three dinners out per month, but skipped the cocktails, drank tap water, had a single glass of wine each and split a dessert for a total of $450 monthly
- Savings, $150 monthly

Yield

Servings	Monthly Savings	10-Year Value × 173	20-Year Value × 521
Hearty	$475	$82,175	$247,475
Light	$150	$25,950	$78,150
Your info			

Great get-togethers, a chance to explore the city and savour some inspiring conversation but now at a new low, low price that allows you to save nearly a quarter of a million dollars over 20 years! That's a feast!

Smoked Cigarettes in a Blackened Lung Sauce

$ $ $ ♉ ♉

Stan's band session at Trevor's place was running late. They were trying to lay down a recording and the sound was all wrong. He hunched over his electric piano, fiddling with some synth controls, his cigarette dangling from his lip. Kim, the guitarist, adjusted the tone controls on her Telecaster and kicked in a different pedal.

Trevor started the recording and tapped his sticks together to set the tempo. "1 and 2 and 3 and 4!"

OK, it was their 14th take but now it was sounding tight! The minor adjustments made the difference. Kim's Fender was growling now and the keys sounded crisp. This was going to be the track!

Stan felt a tickle in his throat. He quietly cleared it, but it was no use. He hacked out a big smoker's cough, his cigarette flying from his mouth. He barked for half a minute straight. The instruments fell silent one by one, leaving just the buzz of the amps and Stan's retching.

The band was steamed; the groove was broken and it was too late to keep going anyway. The bandmates packed up silently. Kim and the bassist left but Stan lingered. Trevor handed him a beer in consolation.

"Dude, you need to lay off the cigs."

"What are you talking about? You smoke all the time."

"Nope. I vape. Big difference."

"What's different?" Stan was skeptical.

"With vaping there is no smoke, no combustion, no carbon monoxide. Just the vapour. You can vape with or without nicotine. Do you hear me cough anymore?"

"Hmm...not recently, I guess. But don't you need to buy pipes and things?"

"I spent about $120 for my pipe up front, but I save $60 each month versus smokes. You should check it out."

A week later they were laying down a perfect track, until Trevor's drumstick flew from his hand 10 bars from the end of the song.

If you smoke, you no doubt receive ample pressure to quit. Forced outside in the dead of winter, well away from building entrances. Lectured by your dentist for yellow teeth and gum disease. Rejected by your friends for the smell and the endless hacking. The insane cost is just the glowing cherry on top of this misery sundae.

Cigarettes are now about $11 a pack, assuming you aren't rolling your own, sailor style. Every year or so, the government tends to add to the taxes, so the math we will do now is conservative, given that we will assume the cost stays fixed. For ease of figuring, we will also leave out increased healthcare costs and just consider the cost of the butts themselves.

Ingredients

- Quit smoking to save your health and maybe even your life as well as an astonishing amount of money.
- See your doctor for advice on the best way to quit.
- Check your employer benefits and programs for help.
- Consider a shift to vaping to save costs, and possibly reduce the health concerns. Check first with your medical professional.

Ask if your employee benefits plan includes smoking cessation clinics.

If someone else in your house smokes, quit together to increase your chance of success.

Hearty Serving

- Household with two smokers
- Each smokes one pack daily for a total cost of $660 monthly
- Both smokers were able to quit entirely
- Savings, $660 monthly

Light Serving

- Single smoker
- Smokes half a pack daily for a cost of $180 monthly
- Switched to vaping for about $86 monthly
- Savings, $94 monthly

Yield

Servings	Monthly Savings	10-Year Value × 173	20-Year Value × 521
Hearty	$660	$114,180	$343,860
Light	$94	$16,262	$48,974
Your info			

The couple in the Hearty Serving example could fund a modest retirement in 20 years simply by quitting smoking! Yes, you could make a case that smoking helps with retirement planning by reducing the number of years of retirement life to fund, but there are tastier routes to financial independence.

The Take-Away Container

Wow, lots of delicious leftovers in this section! The 10 areas we threw on the cutting board can save a potential total of $137,189 for our Light Serving and $396,862 for the Hearty Serving when invested over 10 years:

✓ **Ditch the pricey music downloads.** Look at your total household music costs and save on individual song purchases, subscriptions and even vinyl.

✓ **Consolidate your reading.** Take advantage of free sites with custom information and all-you-can-read magazine apps. Go to the library!

✓ **Stop gambling, start saving.** The surest payoff comes from redirecting your gambling expenses to long-term investments.

✓ **Have fun for less.** Use Groupon, look for discounts and taste some great, lesser-known venues.

✓ **Dump fitness costs in the compost.** Audit your gym memberships and ditch unused and sub-optimized ones. Look at free fitness alternatives.

✓ **Trim TV costs.** Look at HD antennas and other devices to enjoy low-cost entertainment.

✓ **Learn the tricks of discount travel.** Take advantage of comparative information, the sharing economy and other travel tricks.

✓ **Share your toys.** Sell, rent out or share expensive trappings to recoup or split costs. Optimize operating costs.

✓ **Slim down your restaurant spending.** Apply some clever ways to slash the bill but not the fun. Switch some dining out to fun home cooking.

✓ **Butt out.** It's tough to quit, but good to at least look at the economics. Consider vaping.

A bit of creativity and the right resources can open new areas of fun, entertainment and adventure while reducing costs. Check out the Ingredients section at CashflowCookbook.com for tested products and services that can help.

Financial

AH, THE FINAL COURSE. And there are lots of great dishes to choose from. In this section, we look at wealth-generating ideas for all the ways you exchange, transact, invest, borrow and manage your money. Flip through and see which ones are to your taste.

We'll take a closer look at

-    Tax preparation costs
-    Life insurance costs
-    Bank fees
-    Mortgage and debt costs
-    Foreign exchange costs
-    Investment management costs
-    And more

Some of these recipes will be useful right away and others are worth revisiting as the contents of your financial fridge evolve over time.

Cashflow Leeks with Fresh-Squeezed Bank Fees $ ⚕

Bruno was enjoying his regular beer with his buddy Glen. Both squinted at the tiny print on the menus. Both had forgotten their reading glasses, and neither wanted to admit it.

With a little help from the patient waitress, wings and beers were ordered and the conversation turned to business. Glen enjoyed railing at the banking industry as a way of needling Bruno. Bruno smiled and asked what part of banking had him piqued this week.

Glen explained that banking fees were an outrage and that he was paying $30 a month for his premium chequing account.

"Just downgrade to an account with lower fees," shrugged Bruno.

"But I need the travel points, preferred foreign exchange rates and free cheques," countered Glen.

"Why not leave the minimum balance locked into your account?" asked Bruno. "That way they waive the fee."

"You want me to leave $5,000 just sitting in my chequing account not earning anything?" Glen drained his beer.

Bruno did some math on the napkin. "What would you get if you invested that $5,000? Probably not $30 a month. Leave it in there and you're effectively earning 7.2% a year by saving the fee. After tax! Best investment you could make. And you still get the points and whatnot."

Nothing was worse than Bruno being right. Glen focused on gnawing the last bit of goodness from a wing, avoiding eye contact.

If your bank has been snacking on your balance in the form of fees, it may be time to do a bit of cost nibbling of your own.

Look at your last few statements to determine the average monthly cost. Include service fees, costs for Interac transfers, withdrawal fees, fees for printing and mailing a statement, item fees, overdraft fees (yes, you) and whatever else the bank is soaking you for. Do a similar review of your spouse's and kids' accounts. Add up the totals, drop them into the blender and purée them into something more appetizing.

Ingredients

- Book an appointment with your financial institution to review your fees. Ask what they can do to help. You can do this over the phone, but sometimes the in-person approach provides a more comprehensive solution. Be polite and cordial but let them know you are in the process of shopping your financial business and that your search will include other providers.
- Consider looking at all of your financial business and consolidating it with one provider for reduced costs and better service.
- Look online at offerings from other financial institutions, particularly the new branchless banks and credit unions.
- For students, show your student card when setting up accounts. Most institutions offer no-fee accounts for students.

Retail banking is very competitive, particularly if you are a high-net-worth customer. Shop around and ask banks to match competitors' rates and fees.

Hearty Serving

- Family with two adults
- Total monthly account fees, including extra charges, totalling $63
- Moved to more efficient account types for a cost of $24 monthly
- Savings, $39 monthly

Light Serving

- Single adult
- Total monthly account fees, including extra charges, of $24
- Moved to online-only account with no fees
- Savings, $24 monthly

Yield

Servings	Monthly Savings	10-Year Value × 173	20-Year Value × 521
Hearty	$39	$6,747	$20,319
Light	$24	$4,152	$12,504
Your info			

While you're at the bank, preserve this fresh cash by asking the service rep to increase your automated debt payments or savings by an amount equal to your fee reduction.

Fine-Print Filet with a
Credit Card Chiffonade $ Y

Stan checked his credit card balance online and was a bit baffled that the balance was over $400. He didn't recall buying much this month. There were some small charges for groceries, drugstore stuff and home improvement goods. Finally, he saw near the bottom a credit card renewal fee of $150 for his card and another $50 for his partner, Richard's.

He then remembered that months ago they had signed up for the travel rewards card at a mall under heavy pressure from a couple of stubbled, man-bunned youths working at a kiosk. It seemed like a great deal—there were lots of posters of exotic travel destinations and the first year of the card was free, so there was nothing to lose.

Stan sat down and read the fine print of the card agreement and realized the company paid 1.5% in travel rewards on all purchases made on the card. Stan and Richard typically put only $400 or so a month on the card and at 1.5% that earned about $70 in rewards. Subtracting the $200 cost of the cards, they were earning **negative** $130 in travel rewards. Although the posters had said they would be closer than ever to exciting travel, Stan realized that, at this rate, they were actually getting farther away every year they stayed with this card.

Stan called the bank and switched the card to a simple no-fee, no-rewards card that was a better fit for their low-spending lifestyle. Given Stan's long tenure as a bank customer and some gentle persuasion, the bank agreed to reverse the $200 card renewal fee.

Stan used his newfound savings to buy $100 worth of LED lightbulbs to help with ongoing home electricity savings.

With annual interest rates of 20% or more, paying off your credit card(s) every month is *critical*. At 20%, an ongoing $10,000 balance will cost more than $2,000 a year in interest. If you have been in this situation, you know that each month brings new purchases, more interest and an ever-growing balance. It's like a soufflé that starts out OK but then keeps rising and rising, oozing from the oven and taking over the entire kitchen, like something from a cooking horror movie.

Sell things, take a second job, cash in stocks or rent out your basement. Whatever. Just *pay the plastic off every month* and keep the debt soufflé in the oven. With the door firmly closed.

Rant complete. Now let's get the best credit card for your needs.

Ingredients

- When comparing cards, include the annual fee for the primary card and the second (spousal) card.

- Understand the treatment of foreign currency purchases. What mark-up does the card charge beyond the inter-bank rate?

- Ask about the value of the rewards as a percentage of spending. In other words, are they offering 1.5%? 1.75%? 2%? As an example, a card offering $75 in points for every $5,000 of spending is offering $75 ÷ $5,000, or 1.5%. Not as good as a card offering 1.75%.

- Consider the restrictions on using the rewards. Cash rewards don't have blackout periods like travel rewards usually do. Rewards have limited value if you can never use them when you want to.

- Balance reward value against card fees. Can you run your work expenses through your card to up your rewards? If your card fee is $150 and it pays 1.2% in rewards, you need to put $12,500 on your card annually just to cover the card fee. It may be cheaper to get a no-fee card and forgo the rewards.

- Think twice before signing up for the credit card insurance that pays off the balance if you die. Get adequate insurance through conventional life insurance. Better still, don't maintain a balance on your card in the first place.

> Don't sign up for credit cards in malls, airports or other public places, or over the phone. The sales tactics can be aggressive, and occasionally, the sales people aren't always, shall we say, fully informed about the product. Take the time to research several cards online and then select the one that fits your needs, minimizes costs and maximizes rewards.

Hearty Serving

- Two cardholders
- Spending total of $1,667 monthly on cards
- Card fees of $19 monthly
- Card pays 1.2% in rewards, or $20 monthly
- Net benefit, $1 monthly
- Switched to lower-fee card costing equivalent of about $2 monthly and earning 1.75% in rewards
- Began using card for an additional $1,250 in work expenses
- Total rewards now $51 monthly
- Net savings, of $50 monthly

Light Serving

- Single adult
- Spending $225 monthly on card
- Card fee equivalent to $13 monthly for premium travel card
- Card pays 1.5% in rewards, or about $3 monthly
- Net cost, $10 monthly
- Switched to no-fee, no-reward card, saving $13 monthly in card fees and losing the $3 reward
- Net savings, $10 monthly

Yield

Servings	Monthly Savings	10-Year Value × 173	20-Year Value × 521
Hearty	$50	$8,650	$26,050
Light	$10	$1,730	$5,210
Your info			

Note that the monthly net savings represent the improvement from reducing the cost of the cards and/or increasing the reward benefit. Match your card to your spending level so that you are not paying high fees when you can't realize the rewards. Don't buy ingredients you can't cook.

Lightly Poached Life Insurance $ $ 🦃 🦃

Vismaya was reviewing some financial records and noticed that the monthly deductions for her life insurance policy were quite a bit more than the premium stated on the policy. She contacted the insurance company and discovered the additional amount was for policies her ex-husband had taken out on their daughters.

Vismaya could make no sense of the policies since her daughters didn't earn any income that needed to be protected. She contacted Frank, got his agreement, and then cancelled the policies and used the savings to pay off her car loan.

That afternoon, Vismaya was out buying a memory stick for her computer. She approached the cash register and the clerk scanned the device.

"OK so the manufacturer's warranty is only three months on this. Would you like to purchase an additional two years of coverage for only $11?"

"But the memory stick itself is only $35." Vismaya was taken back.

"Well, something could happen..." said the clerk, looking deeply concerned.

"What will happen is that your commission will go up if you sell more memory stick insurance. I will likely lose the thing or run out of capacity before it fails. What could happen to a memory stick?"

"OK, it's up to you. $39.55 please."

Vismaya paid the clerk with her rewards credit card and remembered to get her Air Miles card scanned for a few more points.

Sitting in her car, she did some Googling and found that electronics warranties are rarely claimed by consumers but are a key profit driver at electronics stores. Devices usually become obsolete before they fail. The smart move is to avoid these warranties and to "self-insure" on electronic purchases.

Although saving on the memory stick insurance wouldn't change what was on Vismaya's financial plate, learning that it was a pointless expense would keep her alert to only insuring things that were beyond her capacity to replace.

OK, let's see what's in the life insurance pot.

If you have people who depend on your income, you need a way to protect it if you aren't around. It makes sense to look for ways to save on life insurance, but don't skimp on the coverage itself.

Ingredients

- Research how much insurance you need to cover your funeral cost and replace your income for the balance of your working years.
- Look at your current coverage, both at work and through personal policies.
- Using term life policies with a duration that aligns with your needs is usually the most cost effective.
- It makes little sense to insure children since they have no income to protect. Most people can self-insure to cover funeral costs. If not, look at a small policy to cover those costs.
- Shop the policies online to optimize costs.
- Review your needs as your situation changes—new dependents, paid-off mortgages and health changes may alter your requirements and costs.

Eliminate a policy only if you are certain it is not required or if you have other coverage in place.

Be sure to have adequate disability coverage as well. You are far more likely to become disabled than to die in many age groups.

Don't make your life insurance wholly dependent on your employment; have a policy of your own, in addition to whatever your benefits may offer.

If you want professional help, retain a fee-only financial planner to review your coverage.

Hearty Serving

- Couple with three dependent children
- Have personal policies costing $200 monthly plus coverage through employer
- Retained a financial planner to assess needs, for a one-time fee
- Had more insurance than required between work and personal policies; reduced and re-shopped personal policy online, found that optional extra work insurance was less costly
- Eliminated personal policy, increased work coverage for a new cost of $100 monthly
- Savings, $100 monthly

Light Serving

- Single person with no dependents
- Has work policy providing one times annual salary
- Has additional $200,000 policy (purchased through a friend when she got into the business) costing $50 monthly
- Eliminated the personal policy
- Savings, $50 monthly

Yield

Servings	Monthly Savings	10-Year Value* × 173	20-Year Value* × 521
Hearty	$100	$17,300	$52,100
Light	$50	$8,650	$26,050
Your info			

*You can deduct the one-time fee of the financial planner from the 10- or 20-year value of the savings.

Tax Refund Tartar with Deduction Extract

$ $ 👅 👅

Frank had just visited a tax preparation firm and discovered he qualified for a refund of $2,000. Even better, he paid an extra $130 and the tax-prep guy gave him a cheque on the spot for the value of his refund. He was pleased with himself.

Frank deposited the cheque. His mind was swirling with ideas for spending the newfound cash. It was time to upgrade his home stereo system, and a bigger TV would be great in the living room of his condo. Or he could get some cool new rims and tires for his truck...

Frank strolled into his local diner and sat on a stool at the counter.

"What'll it be?" asked Roxanne.

" Two eggs, sunny side, white toast, bacon, coffee and juice."

"Home fries?"

"Yep! I'm feeling flush."

"Win a lottery?" asked Roxanne, pouring his coffee.

"Nope—got me an instant tax refund, $1,870 in the bank."

"And what did they charge for this instant refund?"

"Just $130."

Roxanne paused for a moment, thinking. "So 6.5% for a two-week loan. That's about 170% a year. Call me next time you need a loan. Your eggs will be right up."

Frank ate his breakfast and wondered how she had done the math that quickly in her head. He settled up and drove to the electronics store to get that TV.

Roxanne mentally calculated the HST on her next three cheques, returned a call from one of her rental property tenants and wondered a) why people paid that much interest on a short-term loan and b) why people paid $15 for a breakfast they could make at home for $3.

OK, exactly how not fun is this? And yet, year after year, here we are, dealing with it. Wasn't all this income tax nonsense supposed to be temporary?

If you are swapping Eurobond futures while trading renaissance art from your Venetian villa, you need a tax expert. If you own a company and need to know how much to dividend to yourself or how to set up a family trust, you will need some competent professional help.

But if your only tax slips are a T4 and an RRSP deduction, you needn't pay a fortune—or indeed anything—to complete your return.

Ingredients

- If you have complex financial affairs, a home business, significant investments and/or a family trust, shop around or ask for referrals for a good accountant. Never skimp on skills, experience or qualifications.

- If your returns are simple—say, a T4, some car deductions and an RRSP contribution slip—look at the free or low-cost online or app tools to complete your return, such as Turbo Tax.

- Resist the immediate cash-back refund offer from tax preparers. Wait two weeks. Eat boiled rice. Hitchhike to work. Borrow from your brother-in-law if you need to. Don't pay the high rates for a two-week loan.

Hearty Serving

- Family with two adults plus three children in university
- Use an accountant charging equivalent of $158 monthly to complete all five returns
- Moved to less-costly, well-qualified accountant charging equivalent of $58 for the returns
- Savings, $100 monthly

Light Serving

- Single adult
- Straightforward tax return
- Using a tax preparation service with immediate cash back for refund
- $120 fee for completing the return and $180 fee for immediate refund of $3,000 totalling equivalent of $25 monthly
- Switched to using free tax-prep software
- Savings, $25 monthly

Yield

Servings	Monthly Savings	10-Year Value × 173	20-Year Value × 521
Hearty	$100	$17,300	$52,100
Light	$25	$4,325	$13,025
Your info			

Instant tax refunds are like instant coffee: convenient but not as good as waiting.

Refried RESP $ $ ⛨

Stan and Richard couldn't believe their daughter, Melissa, was about to have her first birthday. They tried to pare down the guest list, but by the time they included friends and family, Stan's band, his piano students, Richard's office mates and their neighbours, the list was over 80 people.

The big day arrived and people started pouring in. Stan dashed back and forth getting drinks and Richard gathered coats and carried them to the spare room. Stan's parents, Lucy and Brad, held Melissa and tried to organize the traffic of people wanting to see her, comment on her growth and beauty, and predict her future success.

The event was going off without a hitch, but both Stan and Richard noticed something seemed a bit unusual. Richard finally pulled Stan aside and whispered, "OK, this is going to sound weird..."

"I know what you're thinking."

"How could not a single person bring a gift?"

Brad was clinking a glass to gather the attention of the room. "I'm betting that by now, Stan and Richard are wondering why none of us brought gifts." He grinned, catching Stan and Richard red-faced. "I'm afraid I hijacked the mailing list for the party and rechannelled things."

With a big smile, Brad handed Richard an envelope. Richard opened it—it was an RESP for Melissa, with a $2,500 balance already. Richard and Stan were thrilled.

"There are two more gifts," Brad added. "One is the $500 that the government matches and the other is the gift of compound interest. At 7%, and even with no more contributions, at 18, Melissa will have almost $9,500 for university or college. Of course, you will want to contribute each year to take advantage of the grants and compounding."

Everyone applauded. The party was a big success. With no gifts, there was no wrapping paper to clean up and everyone saved trips to the mall. Melissa smiled and burbled as she threw items from the big box of hand-me-down toys the group had gathered for her.

In the Household section we looked at ways to save once your kids are heading off to college or university, but it is also important to look at ways to accumulate the funds. As with any investment, it's best to start early…in this case, right after birth. Or at least as soon as is practical.

Here in Canada, our friends at the federal government have given us a rare delicacy known as the Registered Education Savings Plan. The feds don't give out a lot of free meals so it's worth digging in. Incredibly, only about one-third of Canadians enrolled in post-secondary institutions actually have an RESP.[12] Make sure your kids are among them!

Ingredients
- You can have either a family RESP plan or an individual one for each child.
- There is no annual contribution limit and you can contribute up to $50,000 per child over the lifetime of the plan.
- The government contributes a Canada Education Savings Grant (CESG) of 20% on the first $2,500 contributed each year (i.e., $500), per child, to a lifetime maximum of $7,200 per child. This is free money, people. Eat up.
- Contributions are not tax deductible, but the money grows tax free while in the plan. Earnings are taxed on withdrawal but in the hands of the child, typically netting little or no tax, provided they attend college or university.
- Additional benefits are available for low-income families.
- Full details are available at esdc.gc.ca.

Hearty Serving
- Family with triplets

---

[12] BMO Financial Group study, Sept. 2013.

- Family is eligible for 20% CESG for each of the children ($500 per year per student, lifetime maximum of $7,200 each), for a total value equivalent to $125 monthly

Contributed $208 monthly per student, which grows tax deferred until withdrawal, with the taxable benefit being received in the hands of the (lower-income) student.

Light Serving

- Family with one child
- Family is eligible for 20% CESG ($500 per year, lifetime maximum of $7,200), for a total equivalent to $42 monthly
- Contributed $208 monthly, which grows tax deferred until withdrawal

Yield

Servings	Monthly CESG Grant Value	10-Year Value × 173	15-Year Value* × 316
Hearty	$125	$21,625	$39,500
Light	$42	$7,266	$13,272
Your info			

*We are using just 15 years since that is a typical RESP duration, assuming contributions start at age 2 and end at age 17.

The table ignores the value of the tax-deferred compounding, which is significant but varies with tax bracket and type of investment income. Have an accountant calculate the savings for your situation.

Diced Debt in an
Interest Rate Infusion

Although he held a senior position at the credit union, Bruno liked to spend half a day every month working the front line at a branch to better understand the customers.

As Bruno stood at the wicket, Frank approached and slid his card into the reader. The customer information popped up on Bruno's screen. He scanned the data and noticed Frank owned a condominium with a mortgage and also carried a truck loan.

"Frank, good morning. What can I do for you?" Bruno asked with a slightly forced cheerfulness.

"Hey, Bruno. Surprised to see you out here. Just looking to take out 200 bucks." Frank replied.

"I like to work the front of house now and again," Bruno said. "Let me get that cash for you. Is there anything else I can help you with today?"

"I thought I was pretty clear that I just wanted the 200 bucks."

"Well, I would like to make one suggestion if I may."

"Fine, but I don't have all day."

"I notice you have a truck loan with us at 6.99% as well as a mortgage. Since you have good...well, good-ish, credit, you might qualify for a home equity line of credit secured against your condo, at 2.69%. If we set that up, you could use it to pay off your truck loan and reduce your interest rate by more than half."

"That's the problem with you bankers. Always trying to sell something. I came in looking for 200 bucks. What part wasn't clear?"

Bruno shrugged ever so slightly, handed Frank the $200 and wished him a good day. As he watched him leave, he quickly calculated that on the $28,989 balance on the truck loan, the HELOC at 2.69% would have saved Frank $56 a month and a further $2,016 in interest over the remaining term of the loan. Some people just get what they deserve.

Whether you collect debts like some people collect cookbooks or just carry one or two, there may be an easy way to reduce their cost and, hopefully, send them down the garburator faster.

Build a table that lists all of your debts and add a row for a home equity line of credit from your financial institution. A HELOC is just a loan, secured against a home, that can be used for any purpose.

Here's an example:

Debt	Balance	Interest Rate	Prepayment
Credit card	$5,600	22%	Open
Car loan	$12,500	12%	Open
Mortgage	$246,000	5%	20% / year
HELOC	$0	2.7%	Open

At 22%, that credit card debt is about to boil over and set off the smoke alarm! If you carried the $5,600 for a year, paying only a minimum monthly payment of $112, you would pay $1,221 in interest. And you would still owe $5,477 on the card. That's gotta leave a bad taste.

Ingredients

- If you have a number of debts, talk to your financial institution about a HELOC, and move as much high-interest debt as you can to the lower-cost HELOC.
- If your mortgage allows a 20% annual prepayment, see if you can use the HELOC for the prepayment, to reduce interest costs.
- Of course, always aggressively pay down your highest interest rate loan and be sure to pay off credit card balances each month.

> If you have a home that's worth more than the mortgage on it, you may want to consider a secured HELOC. It will generally involve a few hundred dollars in setup and appraisal fees, but it offers a lower interest rate than an unsecured HELOC.
>
> If you have a stock portfolio and a mortgage or other debt, talk to your accountant or financial advisor about effectively making some or all of your mortgage tax deductible. This can be done by selling some securities to pay off all or part of your mortgage and then borrowing to repurchase the securities.
>
> Don't consolidate all of your debts into a lower-rate HELOC and then start assuming new debts on your credit cards or take out a new car loan.

Hearty Serving

- Family with credit card debt, car loan and mortgage
- Paying interest of $500 monthly on $100,000 of total debt
- Paid off car and credit card and prepaid mortgage using a HELOC, moving $100,000 at average interest of 6% to the HELOC charging 3%
- New interest costs, $250 monthly
- Savings, $250 monthly*

Light Serving

- Family with student loan, credit card debt and car loan
- Total of $30,000 debt at 7%
- Paying $175 monthly
- Arranged debt consolidation loan at 4%
- New interest cost, $100 monthly
- Savings, $75 monthly*

Yield

Servings	Monthly Savings	10-Year Value × 173	20-Year Value × 521
Hearty	$250	$43,250	$130,250
Light	$75	$12,975	$39,075
Your info			

*Canadian mortgages compound semi-annually, whereas most other debts compound monthly, so yes, we are mixing apples and oranges here but the principle is the same.

Debt balances reduce over time so these savings may be high. But you also may take on new debts, making the calculations conservative.

Do the math for your situation. Is there a way to reduce your interest costs? Don't consolidate only to brew up more debt!

Chicken-Fried Foreign Exchange
with Nest Egg Gravy $ $ $ ¥

Vismaya was at the credit union to renew her mortgage and was pleased to see that Bruno, a credit union executive, was working in her branch. Bruno led Vismaya into an office.

"Nice to see you, Vismaya. How can I help?"

"Well, I need to renew my mortgage, but I want to ensure that I'm getting the best possible rate."

"Of course. Let's take a look at your accounts."

Bruno scanned Vismaya's accounts to get the whole picture.

"Hmm, I see you have some US dollar transactions from time to time."

"Yes, I travel to see my brother in Boston."

"OK..." Bruno scrolled through Vismaya's transactions. "It looks like you're converting cash at the airport, paying a high premium for conversions on your credit card and then converting leftover US cash back to Canadian on your return. Expensive!"

"Wow—I never thought of it that way. What do you recommend?"

"How be we set you up with our US package, which includes preferred conversion rates, a US dollar credit card and a US dollar account. We can do all that for only $5 more a month than what you're paying now. It would save you a few hundred dollars a year."

"Sounds like a good idea—and good work on the upsell! Now what about my mortgage?"

"I can take 0.25% off our listed rate on a five-year—that's the best I can do."

"Can you waive the $5 monthly fee on the US account for the first year?"

Bruno smiled, "OK, but no more discounts, no free credit union pens and no free coin wrappers."

Vismaya signed the papers, poured herself a cup of credit union coffee and asked Bruno for some milk and a lid.

OK, so you're up for a bit of jet setting. Or maybe you do some freelancing in a foreign currency or have a kid backpacking in Europe for a few months.

If you regularly find that you need to exchange one currency for another, it is worthwhile to shop for the best exchange rate, just like you would shop for anything else.

Let's compare an airport currency converter, a bank and a discount foreign exchange (FX) company converting 1,000 Canadian dollars to euros and back a few times:

Start with $1,000	Airport FX Kiosk	Bank FX	Discount FX
To euros	€620	€670	€691
Back to $C	$818	$938	$986
Back to euros	€507	€628	€671
Back to $C	$670	$880	$958

Are you likely to switch your money back and forth like this? No. But this exercise shows the difference the exchange rate makes and why you thus want to optimize the rate and do the minimum amount of switching back and forth.

Are you going to rearrange your financial kitchen to exchange $50? No. But if you regularly change money, if you make a large purchase, if you have been blessed with foreign stock options or if a long-lost relative from Colombia has left you an inheritance, it is worth doing some rate shopping.

Ingredients

- Ask your bank about foreign currency accounts and/or options to save on currency conversion fees.

- Look at the currency conversion fees on your credit card—you may want to switch to a card with more attractive conversion rates.

- Consider a foreign currency credit card. For business expenses, have your company reimburse you in the same currency.
- For larger conversions, set up an account with a discount foreign exchange company.

> Look up "Norbert's Gambit," another clever way to convert larger amounts of currency.

Hearty Serving

- Someone receiving foreign stock and travelling out of the country frequently
- Exchanging $2,000 monthly, on average, to a foreign currency and back (two-way conversion)
- Switched from using an airport FX booth to a discount foreign exchange provider
- Savings, $300 monthly

Light Serving

- Someone doing some cross-border travel and making small purchases in foreign currency
- Exchanging $150 monthly (two-way conversion)
- Switched from using an airport FX booth to a discount foreign exchange provider
- Savings, $25 per month

Yield

Servings	Monthly Savings	10-Year Value × 173	20-Year Value × 521
Hearty	$300	$51,900	$156,300
Light	$25	$4,325	$13,025
Your info			

It's worth doing the math. Get these savings on the stove to pay down debt or contribute to your RESP, TFSA or RRSP.

Benefits Bourguignon Simmered in Stock $ $ $ 🍸

With her younger son, Thomas, now more independent, Jodi returned to work managing a group of stores in a large bookstore chain. She enjoyed both the challenges of the role and the opportunity to spend time out of the house with other adults.

The pay was good and it came with a comprehensive benefit package. She didn't pay much attention to the benefits since her husband, Bruno, had a good package at the credit union where he worked.

Despite her busy work schedule, Jodi was still acting as a "taxi mom" to get Thomas to and from his appointments, including one to get a tooth filled.

When Thomas was finished, Jodi reviewed the bill and wondered why she hadn't considered a career in dentistry.

The receptionist noted that Bruno's insurance was on file and then asked Jodi whether she had insurance as well. She indicated that she did, but that her husband already had family coverage.

The receptionist pointed out that Jodi should register her insurance with the dental office as well since her company would cover whatever Bruno's company didn't. On this one appointment, the difference was over $80. Jodi wondered what other benefits she might have missed.

That night Jodi curled up by the fire with the dog by her side, a nice chilled glass of Pinot Grigio and her company benefit handbook. She went in search of hidden gems.

Think back, way back. Weren't you handed some sort of document when you joined the company? Maybe it was a binder or some papers in a folder. Perhaps it was a PDF or a website link with a new password to remember that has to be changed every 30 days and that you aren't supposed to store anywhere and isn't the same as any other password ever used by anyone for anything.

Did you give it a half-hearted browse and then file it? Looked pretty boring on the first pass—insurance this, deductible that, some financial stuff and a rather dull table listing the benefits paid on every conceivable dental procedure. You gave the policy numbers to your dentist and never looked at it again.

Have another look. It may contain some tasty cashflow morsels.

Ingredients

- Take advantage of matching RRSP programs.
- See if there is a beneficial pension plan you can join.
- Enroll in your employee stock purchase plan.
- Look at health benefits beyond the dentist and prescriptions, such as massage therapy, eyeglasses or podiatrists.
- Use reimbursements for gym memberships or fitness gear.
- Look at discounts on other expenses, like car rentals, restaurants or clothing.

And those are just a few examples. Take the time to reread your entire benefit book and see what you have been missing. If you have a working spouse, you may have another book to read. Look for information on coordinating benefits.

Programs like employee stock purchase plans and RRSP matching plans require paycheque deductions, reducing your monthly cashflow. This is why people avoid participating—they have no free cash. *You, however, have in your very hands at this very moment 60 recipes for freeing up the cash you need to take advantage of these great programs.* Note that many of these benefits are taxable, so we will use the after-tax benefits in our calculations.

Hearty Serving

- Two working spouses with benefit programs
- Freed up some cash using other recipes to enable use of financial benefits

- Enrolled in one spouse's stock purchase plan worth 15% of $25,000, or $312 monthly pre-tax (about $187 after tax)
- Made full contribution to one spouse's matching RRSP worth $417 monthly pre-tax (about $250 after tax)
- Claimed extra health benefits of $50 monthly
- Savings, $487 monthly

Light Serving
- Single working adult with a benefit program
- Used stock purchase plan worth 15% of $25,000, or $312 monthly pre-tax (about $187 after tax)
- Claimed extra health benefits of $25 monthly
- Savings, $212 monthly

Yield

Servings	Monthly Benefit	10-Year Value × 173	20-Year Value × 521
Hearty	$487	$84,251	$253,727
Light	$212	$36,676	$110,452
Your info			

Your employee benefits guide might be the second most profitable book you will ever read!

Sparkling Investment Returns in a Low-Cost Sauce $ $ $ 🍷 🍷 🍴 🍴

Brad came into the kitchen one morning to find the table covered in paper and Lucy muttering under her breath. "You're up early," he noted, pouring coffee and clearing a small spot at the table.

"Do you know how our investments have been performing and what we have been paying in fees?" Before Brad could answer, she said "Me either. So, I'm figuring it out. Last year we had a return of 6% after paying over $5,700 in fees on our mutual funds," Lucy said, punching the calculator.

"That's pretty good, isn't it?" asked Brad.

"Not when you consider the market grew 14% last year," countered Lucy. "So I pulled out our records and found that we have been lagging the market consistently for several years."

"Let me get this straight. We are paying nearly six grand a year to be able to consistently lag the market?" Brad was shocked. "I thought I was doing well buying the previous year's top mutual funds."

"I'm not sure that strategy is working," said Lucy. "I'm also not sure if we have the right geographic exposure, the right risk profile or mix of stocks, bonds and cash or that we have things optimized from a tax perspective."

Brad had to agree. "I've been trying to manage it all myself, but it looks like I am in over my head. We should call that financial advisor Jodi recommended."

They retained the well-qualified and highly recommended advisor, who baked them a complete financial cake, setting up investment accounts using individual securities and some low-cost funds with an appropriate mix of bonds, plus Canadian, US and international equity exposure based on their age and risk preferences. Their portfolio also included some dividend growth stocks in their cash account to take advantage of preferential dividend tax treatment.

With these changes, they were now building a better path to their financial future, with costs optimized and the right coaching and investments for their situation. They celebrated their victory by heading out for dinner and then drinks, watching their son Stan and his band perform.

Optimizing the after-cost returns on your investments is critical. There are countless books on how best to invest but it remains a complex subject. Get your apron on and tighten the strings. There is a reason we warmed up on easy recipes like saving on car washes.

Financial advisors will suggest that you need, well, a financial advisor. Purveyors of investing newsletters and tip sheets often suggest that you can enjoy superior returns and save on fees by investing on your own—if you follow the advice you will receive by subscribing to their newsletter. Promoters of actively managed mutual funds suggest their stock-picking prowess is without peer. Robo-advisors imply that machines can outdo humans at asset allocation. And investors who simply track the stock market index often point out that many actively managed equity (stock) funds underperform the market despite charging hefty fees. It's a real witch's brew.

But then there is the reality that investors who manage their own money and invest in mutual funds tend to have returns lower than the funds themselves. How can that be? Because they often mess with them, selling when the world looks scary, then buying them back at a higher price when the future looks brighter. A qualified financial advisor could have coached them through these ups and downs and saved the panicked losses.

Thus, the conundrum. Who is right? We can't begin to boil it down to the right choice for you in a short recipe, but let's at least understand the ingredients and some of the techniques we can use.

Returns Matter

Look at your investment statements for the past several years. Compare your returns against the relevant index. For example, how did your investments in Canadian equities perform compared with the Toronto Stock Exchange Index? Do the same for other investment types (US bonds, US equities, etc.) compared with their relevant indices. The Utensils section in CashflowCookbook.com includes a table of investing returns over time by investment type.

Fees Matter

Next, consider the overall fees you paid for your investments. These include the fees charged by the advisor and the financial institution as well as the fees charged by mutual fund companies. Seemingly small differences in investing costs can make a big difference in your overall returns. For example, imagine that Ken had $100,000 in an RRSP and deposits an additional $10,000 a year for 30 years, earning a 7% return. He invests directly in conservative blue chip stocks and pays negligible fees for the transactions. Ken would retire with an impressive $1.77 million. Not bad!

Now imagine that Ken's friend, Alicia, invested the same amounts but did so using a high-fee mutual fund that held the same stocks but charged annual fees of 2%. Clearly 2% is no big deal. Or is it? Alicia would have only $1.13 million, even though she invested the same amount over the same period. That's a difference of over $640,000, or 37% less than Ken made. Fees *do* matter.

Of course, that assumes that the stocks Ken picks perform as well as the ones in Alicia's mutual funds. It also assumes that both Ken and Alicia won't make any bad decisions, like selling when the market drops and buying back after it rises.

Nothing wrong with paying fees if they are buying you the right kind of advice and coaching. If you are paying high investment fees but still lagging the market consistently over several years, and not getting comprehensive planning and coaching, it's time to take a closer look at who's cooking in your kitchen. Yes, even if the advisor is your sister-in-law. Or you.

Balancing Returns and Costs

What matters is getting the best possible return *after deducting* all investing costs. If you have been lagging the market by several percentage points a year while paying out a total investing cost of, say 2.5%, there is wealth being created. It's just that most of it isn't headed your way. Your sous chef may be eating better than you are.

If your costs are relatively high, but you have been enjoying performance similar to that of the market for several years *after* all the costs, your fees have been well spent—especially if your financial advisor has prepared a detailed financial plan and provided sound tax, estate and other financial advice. Take the time to assess the performance of your investments, after costs, since you began investing. Variations from year to year are less important than your returns over time.

Investment Knowledge

If you have an MBA and have completed the Certified Financial Planner certification, toss this book aside, curl up with a glass of Cabernet and browse the Larousse *Gastronomique*; you probably have a high level of investment knowledge and may be able to assemble a portfolio of investments suitable for your age and risk profile. But as the years go by and your portfolio grows, things will become more complex. Tax considerations become important. There are insurance vehicles that can add to your wealth. You may have registered (TFSA, RRSP, RESP, LIRA)[13] as well as non-registered accounts to manage. You may start on your own but need some help later on.

---

[13] If the acronyms in this recipe are as alien to you as chiltecpín chilis, that alone may suggest that you need some help.

But if you don't know a convertible redeemable preferred from Dutch oven, you have a relatively low level of investing knowledge. Think about how you would score yourself on this measure.

Investing Discipline

If you can weather a market plunge like the one in 2008, if you can think long term and view a market dip as a buying opportunity, you may have a high level of investing discipline. If you can't help but act on that stock tip from your Uber driver with no additional research, you may lack investing discipline.

Let's say the markets had a steep decline, as they do every few years. Would you do some selling just in case this really is Armageddon? Or would you hold tight? Double down and buy more? It's not an easy question when you read the news with dread and, say, 20% of your life savings just disappeared. Again, consider how you might score yourself on this continuum.

Portfolio Size and Complexity

If you are just starting out, you may have just a TFSA with automatic monthly contributions. Once you have maxed that out, the next step might be to do the same with an RRSP account.

At the other end of the spectrum, you may have TSFA, LIRA, RRSP, RESP and cash accounts, with a matching set for your spouse. Managing all of these accounts and ensuring that everything is optimized from a tax, risk, return and cost perspective can be onerous. If you are investing in individual securities, this can be doubly difficult because you need to not only select well but get the right mix and allocation in each type of account.

Let's take a moment to understand some different approaches:

Investing Approaches

Robo-advisors are relatively new. They are services that use your investor risk profile and various market signals to set up and automatically rebalance a basket of exchange-traded funds (ETFs) and/or other securities in an attempt to optimize returns while keeping costs low. This approach typically comes with minimal advice and coaching, tax optimization and retirement planning. It can be a good fit for early stage investors as they start to build a portfolio.

Qualified financial advisors will set up a complete portfolio aligned with the customer's age, risk profile and investment goals. They usually charge a fee that is a percentage of the customer's portfolio value. Their ongoing advice and counsel is particularly important for those with larger portfolios, where complexity, tax consequences and ongoing advice becomes more important. The percentage fee declines with the size of the portfolio and is tax deductible for the non-registered parts of the portfolio. Financial advisors can also add a helpful advice cushion for investors as markets move up and down to prevent panicked selling and reduce exuberance on hot stock tips from Uber drivers.

Fee-only financial planners charge a one-time fee for a service rather than a percentage of the assets in the account. They can produce a complete financial plan, including a retirement blueprint, tax implications and asset allocation models. This approach can be very cost effective for larger accounts. Fee-based planning is useful for those who have the discipline and knowledge to manage their portfolios effectively once the plan is built.

Self-directed accounts can be set up with most financial institutions. They come with few or no fees and allow the account holder to invest in a wide variety of securities, including stocks, bonds, real estate investment trusts (REITs) and options. Success with this model requires a high level of discipline and knowledge and the ability to optimize a portfolio across every measure, including geographic exposure, risk management, mix of securities, tax optimization and life-cycle planning. This approach can become time-consuming and challenging as the portfolio grows in size and complexity.

Ingredients

- Know the returns and costs of your investments to date and monitor them to ensure you can match or exceed market returns over time.

- Understand your investor profile: your age and stage, investment size and complexity, risk profile, investing discipline and investment knowledge.

- Align your investing approach with your investor profile.

- Don't "play" the stock market or act on hot tips or internet- or phone-based solicitations.

- Invest in high-quality securities over the long term with someone (or something in the case of robo-advisors) competently managing your investments. If you have the skills and the discipline, that might be you.

- Ensure that you have competent advice for the initial account setup, but also for annual rebalancing, global asset mix, tax considerations and an optimized mix of holdings in each account type: TFSA, RESP, RRSP and cash accounts.

- Look at setting up a dividend reinvestment plan (DRIP), which allows any earned dividends to be automatically reinvested in the stock that paid the dividend. The great thing about DRIPs is that when the market drops, your dividends will be "buying" more shares—on sale, as it were. As the price rises, your dividends will be buying relatively fewer shares as the price rises.

- Have patience. Compound investing is a powerful force, but it takes time to build results.

> Whatever type of financial advice you select, always take the time to become an educated investor. Read about investing, learn about companies and learn to read financial statements.

Hearty Serving

- $500,000 invested in mutual funds
- Investing cost, 2.4% (fund cost), or $1,000 monthly)
- Switched to lower-cost index funds costing 0.65%, or $271 monthly
- Savings, $729 monthly

Light Serving

- $100,000 invested in mutual funds
- Investing cost, 2.0% (fund cost), or $167 monthly
- Switched to lower-cost investments costing 1.25%, or $104 monthly
- Savings, $63 monthly

Yield

Servings	Monthly Savings	10-Year Value × 173	20-Year Value × 521
Hearty	$729	$126,117	$379,809
Light	$63	$10,899	$32,823
Your info			

This recipe doesn't change your monthly cashflow, but it can provide delicious returns over the long term.

Second Income Sabayon

Stan was chatting with his student Thomas after his piano lesson. Thomas raised the point that he enjoyed the lessons while he was with Stan, but it would be good to have other material to work with, like backing tracks, workbooks, instructional videos of song covers and ear-training tracks. He liked Stan's style of teaching and wanted that same style in other learning aids.

After Thomas left, Stan pondered the idea of somehow building and selling these other materials.

"Great idea," said his partner, Richard. "Once it's set up, it's nearly passive income, which we could use, and it builds your brand as a teacher."

Stan contacted Caroline, one of his students, who was an online marketing and technology whiz. They agreed to swap lesson time for her help with the technology. Caroline set up a system to record video and audio tracks, then built a website and published some of Stan's instructional videos to YouTube.

The YouTube videos built an email list that fed interest to Stan's site, where he offered instructional e-books and the audio and video tracks for sale. Thomas was his first customer for the online materials, picking up some backing tracks and a music theory e-book from Stan's site.

Another benefit was a tremendous pickup in lesson requests, many of them from outside Canada, which he handled over Skype.

These changes transformed Stan's business, yielding new income streams and providing new creative outlets. Over the following months, Stan added more materials for sale, grew his email list and enjoyed watching funds electronically dripping into his account. Musician? Yes. Starving? No!

Most of our recipes have been about reducing the amount you spend as painlessly as possible. But if you want to spice up your debt repayment or layer on assets more quickly, it is worth looking at ways to add another income to your household.

The idea tends to raise objections since it involves, well, more work. Understandable. But might there be a way to earn some extra funds at something you enjoy anyway?

The other issue is that more money means more taxes. True, but it is still more money. And, in 2018 in Ontario, you could earn $11,809 (call it $12,000) and pay no tax whatsoever. So, a non-working spouse could get creative and find something that brings in $1,000 per month and pay no tax. They may benefit further through additional income and extra tax deductions.

Hmm. An extra grand a month to put toward a mortgage or credit card debt is a big deal. And why not do something fun, more like a paying hobby? Discover what lights your stove!

Ingredients
- Start a dog walking business.
- Launch a YouTube channel or blog in your area of interest or expertise and generate ad or affiliate marketing revenue.
- Teach music part time.
- Tutor students on your own or through a tutoring company.
- Teach a course either live or through an online site.
- Sell your craft items online.
- Become an Uber driver.
- Set up a lawn care or snow removal service.
- Rent out a spare room on Airbnb.
- Google "ways to earn extra income" for more examples.
- Claim legitimate business expenses to reduce taxes.

Hearty Serving
- Non-working spouse becomes a dog walker
- Walks two dogs per day at $30 each, 20 days per month, earning $1,200 monthly
- Provides an extra $1,000 monthly net

Light Serving

- Single income earner tutors students part time
- Earns $25 per hour teaching math for 30 hours each month, earning $750 monthly
- Pays 30% tax on this additional income, or $225 monthly
- Provides an extra $525 monthly

Yield

Servings	Monthly Extra Income	10-Year Value × 173	20-Year Value × 521
Hearty	$1,000	$173,000	$521,000
Light	$525	$90,825	$273,525
Your info			

Not exactly crumbs! This is a powerful recipe if one spouse is not working. Depending on your circumstances, it may make more sense to work extra hours, apply for a promotion or get a higher-paying job.

The Take-Away Container

Savings on financial services offer some mighty tasty ways to grow your net worth and save some dough. If you skipped to the end, here are the 10 areas that can save a potential total of $181,823 for our Light Serving and $550,140 for the Hearty Serving—truly a lumberjack breakfast—when invested at 7% over 10 years:

✓ **Deal with your bank fees.** Work with your institution to slice your fees. Comparison shop as well.

✓ **Get the right credit card.** Flambé rewards cards that don't generate enough points to cover the cost of the card.

✓ **Ensure you're insured properly.** Determine the right level of coverage and then shop the policy to optimize the costs.

✓ **Stop paying for instant-refund tax services.** Do your own return using tax software if you have a basic return.

✓ **Max out education support.** Take advantage of free entrées from the government and tax-deferred education investments in an RESP.

✓ **Downsize your debt costs.** Set the table with a list of your debts. Reduce borrowing costs with a HELOC.

✓ **Exchange the exchange rate.** Boil down currency costs through fewer transactions and optimized exchange rates.

✓ **Understand your benefits.** Study your and your spouse's benefits to take full advantage of the offerings.

✓ **Optimize investment returns and fees.** Ensure you are getting both a great return after fees and the right advice.

✓ **Do the side hustle.** A non-working spouse can whip up a small business and earn more than $11,000 tax free.

Take the time to learn about the costs related to the management of your finances. Learn to optimize them; they are often hidden, but they are expenditures like any other.

Overall Summary: The Stock Pot

WE'VE HAD A LOT OF POTS ON THE STOVE. Let's summarize the cash value of these dishes. Below are all the categories and their value over just 10 years for Hearty and Light Servings. Fill in your results on the right. How did you do?

Category	Hearty Serving Total	Light Serving Total	Your Total
Housing	$327,598	$104,039	
Transportation	320,223	112,796	
Food & Drink	359,494	84,251	
Household	432,327	158,468	
Lifestyle	396,862	137,189	
Financials	550,140	181,823	
Total	$2,386,644	$778,566	

Hopefully you found some room for improvement and have the savings working for you to pare down debt and get your investments rising. Maybe you have even changed the way you look at your finances.

With that complete, we need to ask that critical culinary question: Did you leave any room for dessert?

Epilogue

JODI AND BRUNO RETIRED TOGETHER and moved to a small chalet where they enjoyed skiing in the winter and sailing and biking in the summer. Their two sons visit frequently. Ken became a history professor at Dalhousie University. Thomas continued studying piano and was accepted into the Juilliard School of Music in New York. By optimizing their expenditures, the whole family was able to end their financial worries and enjoy all that life has to offer.

Brad and Lucy celebrated their 60th anniversary. Not long after, Brad passed away in his sleep and Lucy soon moved into a retirement home. She gave the family home to their son, Stan, to use for his music studios and lessons to help the next generation enjoy the gift of music.

Stan and Richard renovated their red brick house, but eventually had to move away from the constant rumble of the train tracks. Stan became a YouTube sensation with his online piano programs and Richard was promoted to chief operating officer of his engineering firm. Their investments outpaced their expenses and they were able to establish an orphanage in their daughter Melissa's war-torn homeland. Melissa spent summers working there during university.

William and Vismaya eloped to Boston and enjoyed time with her relatives there. They lived an active vegan lifestyle and William helped raise Vismaya's two daughters. Serena overcame her early procrastination and became a noted cardiac surgeon; Caroline became an architect in Calgary and redefined the skyline with her innovative designs. They enjoyed family vacations at Airbnbs, lodging in exotic destinations.

Frank was convicted of fraud in relation to some of his construction projects. He is still spending his days within the confines of one of our nation's older and less-comfortable medium-security institutions, where he was barred from privileges in the prison workshop because of shoddy workmanship. With everything provided for him, even he was able to enjoy financial independence, if only until the end of his sentence, when he will need to face his debts, including quite a bit of accrued interest.

Cashflow Cookbook: The Website

ONCE YOU'VE COMPLETED THE RECIPES in this book, you may have a craving for a little more, like a cappuccino after a nice dinner. Whatever you want next in your personal finance journey, it's a click away at CashflowCookbook.com. Here's what to expect when you get there:

Blog: You just read a few dozen recipes that can send your monthly recurring expenses to the chopping block. Each recipe began with a short story that included a mini-recipe, kind of like an appetizer.

At CashflowCookbook.com you will find new "Appetizers" in the blog each month. Appetizers are lighter ideas, often providing one-time savings that are a nice complement to the recipes in the book. Subscribe on the site to get them right to your inbox for free.

Subscribe: No spam. No useless offers. No selling the subscriber list to anyone. Subscribers get the new appetizers (blog posts) served to their inbox each month. As new editions and complementary information becomes available, you'll hear about that as well. But it's all at a nice pace—maybe two or three emails a month. And it's easy to unsubscribe.

Utensils: If you need some help building debt sheets or net worth sheets in Excel, want to use different future value factors or otherwise need help to implement the recipes in the book, the Utensils section is there for you. You can download a table that shows you returns for different types of investments over time. Are your investments ahead or behind the index? Other tools will follow. Check it out and download what you need, all for free.

Ingredients: At Cashflow Cookbook, we are always looking for fresh ideas to help serve up a tastier financial future. We sometimes discover products or services that can help. Worthwhile ones are added to the Ingredients section at CashflowCookbook.com. They don't get added unless they are reputable and tested. We don't accept payment to list offerings, but we may get a referral fee if you check out or buy these products and services.

If you have ideas for content or other recipes, please comment on the blog or send me your thoughts:
gord@CashflowCookbook.com.

Acknowledgements

A BIG THANKS to everyone who has been a part of this book.

Special thanks to my developmental editor, Elizabeth Williams of BizMarketer.org, who spiced up the prose and trimmed the fat throughout, and my copy editor, Donna Dawson. Austin Stein added another helping of editorial support. Scott Kish of KishStudio.com baked the signature hat and the icons. Connor Stein cooked up the website and added a dash of youthful perspective to the content. Simon Gladstone took the site further and added some great functionality.

Thanks to everyone who gave the ideas a stir, including Paul Atkinson, Sandy Di Felice, Mike Dunn, Brent Broadhurst, Jim Eplett, Mike Fox, Gurmit Gill, Rolie Hamar, Greg Johnston, Mark Kindrachuk, Kerry Mitchell, Roxanne Pearce, Caleb Rubin, David Sculthorpe, Mark Stevenson, Katie Spiler, Joel Teitelbaum and Lucy Vasic. Special thanks to Peter Foulds, who found the car wash receipt that started this whole thing.

Finally, none of this would be possible without the ongoing support of my family. Thanks for helping me throughout this financial feast.

Public Speaking

I AM PASSIONATE ABOUT helping people improve their finances and am interested in speaking to groups like these:

- Company employees, to help them learn about financial wellness and reducing their money stress
- Clients of financial advisors, to help them free up funds for incremental investment contributions to build wealth
- Clients of debt management companies, to help them find creative ways to free up funds for debt repayment

I am also available to present keynote speeches for company, industry and trade events.

For booking availability, fees and other information, please email speaking@CashflowCookbook.com.

For TV, radio, press and podcast appearances, please send an overview of the program, audience and timing to media@Cashflow-Cookbook.com.

Order more copies of

Cashflow Cookbook

Free Express Shipping

Order online at CashflowCookbook.com or email completed form to orders@CashflowCookbook.com.

Name:_____

Address: _____

City: _____ State/Province _____

Zip/Postal code: _____ Phone: _____

Email: _____

Ship to (if different from above):

Name: _____

Address: _____

City: _____ State/Province _____

Zip/Postal code: _____ Phone: _____

Email: _____

Quantity ordered: _____ × $24.95* = _____

Canadian residents add 5% GST. Books ship FREE the day orders are received and typically arrive within 2–5 business days.

Credit card type: Visa _____ MasterCard _____

Credit card #: _____

Expiry date: _____

Name on card: _____

Signature: _____